# THE INDEPENDENT GUIDE TO DISNEYLAND PARIS 2015
# 4th EDITION

Limit of Liability and Disclaimer of Warranty: The publisher has used its best efforts in preparing this book, and the information provided herein is provided "as is." Independent Guides and the author make no representation or warranties with respect to the accuracy or completeness of the contents of this book and specifically disclaims any implied warranties of merchantability or fitness for any particular purpose and shall in no event be liable for any loss of profit or any other commercial damage, including but not limited to special, incidental, consequential, or other damages. Please read all signs before entering attractions, as well as the terms and conditions of any third party companies used. Prices are approximate, and do fluctuate.

Copyright Notice:
Contents copyright (C) 2012-2015 Independent Guides. All rights reserved. No part of this document or the related files may be reproduced or transmitted in any form, by any means (electronic, photocopying, recording, or otherwise) without the prior written permission of the publisher, unless it is for personal use. Some images and text copyright (C) The Walt Disney Company and its affiliates and subsidiaries. This guide is not a The Walt Disney Company product, not is it endorsed by said company.

# TABLE OF CONTENTS:

**Guide Intro** .................................................................... **5**

**Introduction to Disneyland Paris** ................................ **6**

**Planning your trip** ......................................................... **7**

**Getting there** ................................................................ **10**
    Eurostar: ............................................................................. 10
    Eurotunnel (from UK): ..................................................... 16
    Ferry (from UK): ............................................................... 17

**The Hotels:** ................................................................... **18**
    Official Disney Hotels: ..................................................... 18
    Partner Hotels: .................................................................. 31

**Tickets** .......................................................................... **39**
    Buying Tickets At The Park Gates: ................................. 39
    Online: ................................................................................ 40
    Vouchers: ........................................................................... 42
    Ticket Tips: ........................................................................ 43
    Annual Passports: ............................................................ 44

**Disneyland Park** ......................................................... **47**
    Main Street U.S.A: ............................................................ 48
    Frontierland: ..................................................................... 50
    Adventureland: ................................................................. 55
    Fantasyland: ...................................................................... 59
    Discoveryland: .................................................................. 70
    Fireworks in Disneyland Park – Disney Dreams: ........ 78
    Disney Dreams Viewing Guide: ..................................... 79
    Parades: ............................................................................. 82

**Walt Disney Studios Park** ......................................... **84**
    Front Lot: ........................................................................... 85
    Production Courtyard: .................................................... 85
    Backlot: .............................................................................. 91
    Toon Studio: ...................................................................... 95
    Toy Story Playland: ......................................................... 101

**Fastpass** ..................................................................... **104**
    How to use Fastpass at Disneyland Paris: .................. 104

- List of FASTPASS attractions: ............................................................. 105
- Extra tips: ............................................................................................. 106
- Special Fastpass tickets: .................................................................... 108

## Disney Village ..................................................................... 109
- Entertainment: ..................................................................................... 109
- Restaurants: ......................................................................................... 113
- Shops: ................................................................................................. 115

## Touring Plans ..................................................................... 117
- Disneyland Park: .................................................................................. 118
- Walt Disney Studios Park: ................................................................... 124

## Outside The Parks ............................................................. 126

## Guests with Disabilities: ................................................... 130

## Meeting The Characters ................................................... 135

## Doing Disney on a budget ................................................. 139

## Dining .................................................................................. 143
- Meal Plans: .......................................................................................... 144
- Making Reservations: ......................................................................... 148
- Tipping in Restaurants: ...................................................................... 149

## Useful to know ................................................................... 150
- When to visit: ...................................................................................... 150
- Mobile phone apps: ............................................................................ 153
- On-ride photos: ................................................................................... 153
- Photopass: .......................................................................................... 154
- Photopass+ ......................................................................................... 155
- Baby Switch and Rider Switch: .......................................................... 157
- Parking: ............................................................................................... 157
- Single Rider Queue Lines: ................................................................. 158
- Extra Magic Hours: ............................................................................. 159

## How to spend less time queuing ...................................... 168

## Disneyland Paris for Walt Disney World Regulars .......... 171

## Seasonal Changes & The Future ...................................... 178

**Chapter 1**
# Guide Intro

We would like to begin with a big "thank you" for purchasing The Independent Guide to Disneyland Paris 2015. This guide includes all sorts of kinds information that will enhance your visit to Disneyland Paris. You will find time saving tips, ways to save money, details on restaurants and attractions, touring plans, and much more. This guide's aim is to be easy to read and comprehensive, covering every aspect of your trip to Disneyland Paris.

There is no paid-for advertising in this guide - it is completely independent and we have not been paid for any of these opinions by Disneyland Paris or any other company mentioned herein. Some of the links we include in this guide are affiliate links which help us to keep running – if you use our links we will get a small percentage of your purchases at no extra cost to you.

As well as being a regular guest, the author has also worked as a Cast Member at Disneyland Paris and therefore has experienced the parks year round, from the busiest day to the quietest. As such, there as "Top Tips" scattered throughout the book with hidden secrets and important information.

We recommend you read the entire guide before you start planning your holiday, then follow our guide to planning your trip, and finish by bookmarking sections for when you are in the parks.

If you have any questions about the guide or the parks please contact us directly at info@dlparisguide.com.

Chapter 2
# Introduction to Disneyland Paris

Disneyland Paris is Europe's most popular destination, having amassed over 250 million visitors in just twenty years: faster than any other Disney theme park ever.

The project for the resort started in the 1980s when Disney executives wanted to bring the magic of Disney theme parks over to Europe where the original stories, which inspire many Disney fairytales, originate. They soon decided on constructing the resort in France due to its central location and favourable weather when compared to some countries further north in Europe. The fact that the location was less than a two-hour flight from much of Europe sealed the deal.

Disneyland Park opened in 1992 as a European recreation of California's Disneyland. Over the years, the park has expanded with new rides and experiences. In 2002, Walt Disney Studios Park opened its doors right next door. It became the second park at the resort, providing a portal for movie fanatics. As well as the two theme parks, guests can enjoy the Disney Village area which does not require an admission fee – here you will find shopping and dining experiences that cover a wide range of tastes. A golf course, a campsite with an adventure playground and seven themed hotels are all also accessible to guests.

In 2015, the resort celebrates its 23$^{rd}$ anniversary and the Cast Members at Disneyland Paris are already preparing for the 25$^{th}$-year celebrations. Disneyland Paris is not just a theme park resort; it is a place where dreams really do come true for thousands of guests every single day.

**Chapter 3**
# Planning your trip

1. Planning a trip to Disneyland Paris may seem daunting. You have to think about transport, accommodation, food, park tickets, how much money to take, etc. This section aims to get you prepared by following the steps below. All of these steps are further developed in the chapters that follow in this guide.

2. Decide how you want to get to the resort – will you be flying, driving or taking a train? If you will be using public transportation be sure to check what time you will arrive at the resort and when you will be leaving, so that you can plan your days accordingly.

3. If you can, decide whether you will be going back more than once in the next year. If you will be, then consider getting an annual passport instead of buying park entry tickets. There is more information on annual passes later in this book.

4. Decide whether you want to stay on-site or off-site. On-site packages mean you get the hotel and your park tickets all for one price. Staying off-site usually means that you pay for the hotels and your park tickets separately and that you will stay at a non-Disney owned hotel. This may work out cheaper if you are not planning on visiting the theme parks every day.
5. Get park maps before you go - Go on eBay and buy the latest park maps or print the maps off the official website. Combine the park maps with the guide to the parks in this book and decide which attractions and shows you want to experience. We recommend you circle the ones you definitely to visit on your map, or simply write them down. Having an idea of what park different attractions are in, as well as a general sense of where they are located is essential to making the most of your time whilst you are there. You do not have to memorise the map, but looking at it in advance will save you some valuable time when you arrive.
6. Check the opening hours of the theme parks. Park opening hours vary wildly, the parks can open as early as 8:00am and close as late as 1:00am on certain days of the year. The latest hours are on our website here -
http://www.independentguidebooks.com/dlp/hours
7. Be aware of refurbishments – As Disneyland Paris is open 365 days a year, it does not have a set period of the year to perform its maintenance like most other theme parks do. Instead, Disneyland Paris closes certain rides for refurbishment throughout the year. This is usually done once a year per ride and the resort tries to do this during periods of low attendance to limit the impact on guests. Refurbishments are usually published a couple of months in advance. If there is a particular attraction you want to experience, make sure to check out the refurbishment schedule on our website -
http://www.independentguidebooks.com/dlp/refurbs

8. Download the Times Guide – The Times Guide tell you when the parades and shows are taking place, and when the characters are set to appear. The schedule for your trip can be seen up to two weeks in advance here: http://www.disneylandparis.co.uk/entertainment/shows-and-parades-in-disneyland-parks/ .
9. Read through the whole of this guide thoroughly, screenshot and print out key pages, or take it with you on your e-reader, tablet or mobile phone.
10. Check our website www.independentguidebooks.com/dlp/ for any updates before leaving.
11. If you are travelling from outside Continental Europe, be sure to bring plug adapters, as sockets in France may differ from your home country.
12. Make sure you get your Euros in advance. Do not rely on buying it at the airport or train station. We recommend getting a pre-paid currency card that you can top up. For UK users we recommend FairFx's service. There is usually a £9.95 fee for the card but by using this special link you get the card for free: http://bit.ly/debitdlp

Chapter 4
# Getting there

Traveling to Disneyland Paris is simple due to its central location; it is about two hours away from most of Europe. Options include driving, flying and high-speed trains.

## Eurostar:
## Direct from the UK:

The Eurostar is perhaps the easiest option for people from the south of the UK allowing you to reach the doorstep of Disneyland Paris direct in just 2 hours 42 minutes from London, and even less from Ebbsfleet and Ashford. Prices *start* at £69 per adult return. There is one direct train per day that leaves London at 10:15 (London time) and arrives at 13:57 (Paris time) at Marne la Vallée-Chessy Station (Disneyland). There are no direct trains on Tuesdays and Saturdays, except during British school holidays. Return direct trains depart Disneyland Paris at 18:02.

The direct Eurostar service is incredibly convenient with security and check-in usually able to be completed in less than five minutes. We do however notice that the trains are starting to show their age. Currently, there is no Wi-Fi on board the trains either. Having contacted Eurostar regarding this we were informed that the existing trains are "currently undergoing a program of refurbishment, and these are due for delivery over the next few years." Eurostar also told us that the first new e320 trains will be delivered at the end of 2015. Both the new and refurbished trains will be equipped with Wi-Fi and feature redesigned and refreshed interiors bringing the trains into the 21$^{st}$ century.

## Indirect from the UK:

The direct Eurostar service does not provide much flexibility with only one train per day in each direction. Visitors who prefer to arrive at Disneyland Paris earlier in the day, or who want a later train, have the possibility to do so with the indirect 'Eurostar + TGV' option.

Indirect trains are usually bound for Brussels. Passengers board a Eurostar train as usual in the UK and disembark at Lille Europe station, which is about 1 hour and 20 minutes from London. At Lille Europe, passengers wait for their connecting TGV train from Lille Europe to Marne la Vallée - Chessy Station (Disneyland). The journey takes as little as 3h03m with a 28-minute stopover.

Indirect trains can be a good option if there are no direct Eurostar trains available. It can also work out cheaper if you do not mind adding an extra 30-60 minutes of journey time in each direction. Furthermore, it allows you added flexibility, as there are several trains every day from the UK to Lille Europe, and then from Lille Europe to Disneyland, as opposed to the one train per day of the direct service.

As an example, getting the 08:04 Eurostar to Lille and then changing at Lille will mean you arrive at 12:07 (Paris time), which should allow plenty of time to spend in the parks. Changing trains is very easy to do and 30 minutes is plenty of time. Just check that you are on the right train at the platform as there are often multiple trains on the same platform at the same time. The TGV train that takes you from Lille will most likely make several stops and only stop at Marne-La-Vallee - Chessy (Disneyland Paris) for a minute or two so make sure you do not miss your stop as it is not the end of the route. There is a very helpful video guide available on YouTube from DreamTravelGroup entitled "Eurostar to Disneyland Paris changing at Lille... no problem!" You can find this video here: http://bit.ly/dlplille

## Eurostar + RER (from central Paris):

Disneyland Paris is actually located about 32km from the centre of Paris so arriving in central Paris means you are still quite a journey away from Disneyland Paris. This option does however offer you an incredible amount of flexibility as far as timing is concerned. It is possible to a Eurostar to central Paris - Gare du Nord station and then get a regional (RER) train to Marne-la-Vallee – Chessy (Disneyland Paris).

A direct London to Paris Eurostar service has a journey time of 2h15m with up to 24 trains running between the two cities every day.

From the moment when you arrive at Paris – Gare du Nord station by Eurostar, you will take a further 50 to 60 minutes in travel time to reach Disneyland Paris - a ticket on the Paris train system to Disneyland Paris will cost you about €7.50 per adult and half that for a child under 10 years old. Follow the signs at Gare du Nord, to the 'Metro and RER' trains. Take the RER B line in direction of Robinson, Antony or Saine Rémy-lès-Chevreuse for one stop to "Chatelet-Les Halles." Here you transfer to RER A by simply going to the otherside of the platform and get on a train going in the direction of Marne La Vallée-Chessy. Use the overhead information boards to verify that the train will indeed be going to Marne La Vallee – Chessy station. If it will, there should be a light illuminated next to the station's name. Marne La Vallée - Chessy (Disneyland) is the last stop on the RER A line. This train journey takes about 40 minutes.

**Top Tip**: Do not book your Eurostar travel through Disneyland Paris as part of a package without checking prices direct with Eurostar first. It often works out significantly more expensive to book transportation with Disneyland Paris. Instead we recommend you book your train direct at www.eurostar.com where you can get discounts the earlier you book. However, when Disney has an offer such as free travel for children it can be significantly cheaper to book with Disneyland Paris. As such, we recommend you check both options. You can book Eurostar trains between 3 and 6 months in advance, depending on the season and route.

When arriving from the Eurostar at "Marne La Vallee - Chessy": Leave the station by taking the escalator up, turn left through the glass barrier and exit the station straight ahead.
Turn right outside the station. It is a 30-second walk to the Disney Village and a two-minute walk to the two theme parks.
If you turn left outside the station, you will find the free shuttle buses to the hotels in the area - just follow the signs in the station. There are a few small shops and cafes in the station that sell food at prices much cheaper than in the parks. There is also a minimarket. There is a paid "left luggage" service on the upper floor of the station.

**Disney Express luggage service:**
If you have booked the Eurostar journey as part of a package with Disneyland Paris directly, you will have Disney Express luggage transfer included. Simply follow the signs to the Disney Express counters, located on the upper level of the station and find the Cast Member behind the desk for your particular hotel. You will check in for your hotel there, be given your park tickets, meals vouchers (if ordered) and any other documentation. You leave your luggage with the Cast Members at these desks. Your bags will be taken to your hotel by Disney and stored in luggage storage. Now, you are free to go and explore the parks and get your luggage later at your hotel!

On the direct Eurostar service from the UK, Disney Cast Members will pass through the train to explain the Disney Express baggage service and confirm your hotel check-in. Despite this, you will still need to visit the Disney Express counter to leave your luggage.

If you have not booked the Eurostar through Disney, you can add the Disney Express luggage transfer service to your booking through your travel agent or Disney directly in advance for a cost of £16 or €16 return per adult. You can do this at the time of booking. The service is free for every child accompanying a paying adult. Queues for the Disney Express can sometimes be long after a train arrives so it is worth being brisk getting off the train. This service is available on both direct and indirect Eurostar services, as well as for others arriving via TGV or by other means at the station. The Disney Express counter is located on the top floor of Marne La Vallee - Chessy Station and is open from 8:00am to 9:30pm, 7 days a week.

## Plane:

Flying to Paris is convenient for most of the UK and Europe, as well as other visitors from all across the world. A direct flight from London to Paris is about 1 hour, and from Birmingham/Manchester is about 1 hour 30mins. The French capital is also under two hours away from most of Europe. Flights with low cost airlines start at around £50 from London, £80 from Birmingham and £100 from York each way. Paris has three airports you fly into:

- **Charles-de-Gaulle Airport** - This is the main Parisian airport and the largest.
    - **By Train**: From the airport you can catch a direct TGV train service, which takes between 9 and 12 minutes from Terminal 2 to Marne-La-Vallee - Chessy (Disneyland) station. Tickets can be pre-booked online at http://www.voyages-sncf.com, however we recommend that you simply book them when you arrive at the airport, which avoids you missing any pre-booked trains. Tickets are priced at about €20 to €25 per person each way. The first train starts at approximately 7:00am. There are no direct

TGV trains after about 21:19 (though be sure to check the schedule online by doing a test booking on voyages-sncf.com).
- o **By Coach**: The Magical Shuttle bus can be taken from the airport to the resort and even directly to many of the local Disneyland area hotels. It also makes return journeys to the airport. There are 13-14 journeys in each direction throughout the day. The price is about €20 per adult each way and €16 per child ages 3-11. The journey takes approximately 1 hour and 35 minutes each way. Book at www.independentguidebooks.com/magicalshuttle.
- o **By Taxi**: A taxi is around €90-€100 each way for a family of four. This may work out as being the cheapest and more convenient option for large groups.
- o **By Public Transport**: Get the RER B to *Chatelet les Halles* station, then switch to RER A to *Marne La Vallee – Chessy*. This will cost approximately €16 per adult with a travel time of around 1 hour 30 minutes. Children under 10 years of age pay half price, and children under 4 years travel for free.

- **Orly Airport**
  - o **By Coach**: The Magical Shuttle bus costs €20 per adult each way, and children can travel for €16 each way. Coach transfers take approximately 1 hour and 35 minutes each way. Book at www.independentguidebooks.com/magicalshuttle.
  - o **By Public Transport**: Get the Orlyval train (approx. €10 per adult - Runs 6:00am to 11:00pm) to *Antony Orlyval* station. From *Antony Orlyval* take the RER B to central Paris and *Chatelet-Les Halles* station. From here you get the RER A to *Marne la Vallee – Chessy* station (Disneyland). The total journey time is approximately 1 hour and 30 minutes.
  - o **By Taxi/Private Van**: Prices vary between €80 and €135 for parties of 3 to 8 people. This can be the cheapest and most comfortable option depending on

group size.
- **Beauvais-Tille Airport**
    - **By Coach**: The Magical Shuttle bus costs €24 per person each way regardless of age (children under 3 travel for free). To be honest, we do not recommend landing at this airport for Disneyland Paris. The shuttle trips take between 2 hours and 30 minutes and 3 hours and 30 minutes each way. The shuttle will also stop at Charles de Gaulle airport along the route. Book at www.independentguidebooks.com/magicalshuttle.
    - **By Taxi:** The taxi fare is approximately €180-€200 each way. Due to the high price we would recommend renting a car in this case instead of using a taxi.

## Eurotunnel (from UK): Driving Directions

The Eurotunnel is a specially designed train travel service that allows passengers and vehicles to travel together from Folkestone (England) and arrive in Calais (France) in only 35 minutes. From Calais (France) it is approximately a three-and-a-half hour drive to Disneyland Paris. Take the A26 towards Arras passing through St. Omer. There take the A1 (also known at the Autoroute du Nord or E15) towards Paris. Take exit 6 after Charles de Gaulle Airport, onto the A104. This will take you to the A4, follow this road and exit 14 is Disneyland Paris. This journey will cost approximately €20 in tolls and approximately €30 in fuel each way.

## Ferry (from UK): Driving Directions

You can also take your car on the ferry from Dover (England) to Calais (France). P&O Ferries, for example, is one of the most popular companies. The ferry crossing is often cheaper than the Eurotunnel but it also takes about 90 minutes, almost three times as long. From Calais (France) it is approximately a three-and-a-half hour drive to Disneyland Paris. Take the A26 towards Arras passing through St. Omer. There take the A1 (also known at the AutoRoute du Nord or E15) towards Paris.
Take exit 6 after Charles de Gaulle Airport, onto the A104. This will take you to the A4, follow this road and exit 14 is Disneyland Paris. The journey will cost approximately €20 each way in tolls.

## The Law

If driving, please be aware that French law requires all drivers to have a reflective jacket on display in your vehicle at all times in case of an emergency. You must also carry a warning triangle and a personal breathalyser in the boot of your car. If the car you will be driving comes from the UK, where they drive on the left, then you will also need to purchase headlight beam changers. These are stickers that you apply to your headlights and change the direction of the beam, so that they do not dazzle drivers in France. Check for any other applicable driving laws before you leave. You will need to pay tollbooths of approximately €20 each way from Calais to Disneyland Paris.

Chapter 5

# The Hotels:
## Official Disney Hotels:
Disneyland Paris owns and operates seven on-site hotels, each themed to represent a part of America – one is even a campsite where you can stay in log cabins. When booking a hotel stay directly with Disneyland Paris, your hotel price will include park entry tickets as well as breakfast (unless otherwise stated).

### Advantages of staying at Disneyland Paris hotel:
- A front-desk staffed 24 hours a day
- Friendly Cast Members with a knowledge of the whole resort
- The ability to make dining reservations in person without having to leave your hotel
- Detailed theming and total immersion
- A stay in the heart of the Disney magic
- Extra Magic Hours – available daily. EMHs allow hotel guests entry into selected parts of Disneyland Park two hours before general guests meaning attraction wait times are either very low or non existent.
- A short distance to the theme parks – a 20-minute walk or less.
- Free shuttle service from all the hotels to the theme parks (except Davy Crockett Ranch)
- An all-you-can-eat continental breakfast is included with every hotel room booked through Disney (except at Davy Crockett Ranch).
- Disney Shopping Service - if you buy some merchandise in the parks before 3:00pm you can have it delivered to your hotel to be collected in the evening leaving your hands free.
- Park tickets are included in all reservations unless otherwise stated

**Top Tip:** When checking in, you will have the choice of when you would like to eat your breakfast. If you can, choose the 7:00am or 7:30am time slot as from 8:00am onwards the breakfast area becomes very busy with queues to even get in.

**Top Tip 2**: Your arrival date determines the price for your entire stay (e.g. If you arrive on a date within the Value pricing season and the remaining days of your holiday are in the Moderate pricing season, your stay will be charged at the Value pricing season). However, this can also work against you where your arrival date could be in High season and then your other nights in the Regular season and you will pay the High season rate for the entire duration.

There are two solutions: change your dates, or book one package for the more expensive night(s) and then another package for the cheaper remaining night(s) but you may have to leave your room and re-check in with this solution. It is worth mentioning it to the Cast Members to see if you can keep your room. To see what season you will arrive in, download the brochure from the Disneyland Paris website at www.disneylandparis.co.uk. A booking advisor may be able to advise what the best option for you is if you book over the phone.

**Important Note**: Since November 2014 the Disney hotels no longer feature characters in their breakfast areas as they did previously. Instead, guests can now find characters at Disneyland Park during Extra Magic Hours.

**Pricing Information:** Room prices in this section are based on arrivals between April 2015 and Mars 2016 for one night only – multiple night stays carry a lower "per night" cost. The per-night cost after the third night is 45% to 85% cheaper, as most visitors will not need more than four days to visit the resort. This can make a longer stay at the hotels much better value for money overall.

# Disneyland Hotel:

**Theme:** Art Deco / Victorian

**Transport:** Located at the entrance to Disneyland Park, and a 3-minute walk to Walt Disney Studios Park.

**Number of rooms:** 565 rooms, including 27 suites.

**Room size:** 34 square metres for standard rooms (up to 4 people, plus one child under 3 years old in a cot), and 58 square metres in the Castle Club Suites (there are different sized suites available at up to 187 square metres – these can only be booked by phone. This includes the luxury Sleeping Beauty suite, the Cinderella suite, Tinker Bell suite and Walt's Apartment Suite). Family rooms (up to 5 people with one on a sofa bed), and Castle Club rooms (up to 4 people – these can only be booked by phone) are also available.

**Breakfast**: Included. The buffet breakfast at this hotel has the widest selection of food items.

**Room prices:** €376 to €706 per person per night for a standard room based on 2 adults sharing. A Castle Club standard room is priced at €501 to €861 per person per night.

**Activities:** An indoor pool, sauna and/or steam bath and a fitness suite are all available for guests of this hotel free of charge. A spa with a massaging service is also available for an extra fee. A 'Princess for a day' experience is also available for an additional charge transforming your little girl into a princess with a dress, make-up, accessories and more (Make up and hairstyle only - €50, Make up and hairstyle and dress - €100). A "Club Minnie" Playroom, children's corner, and a video game arcade are also available. Dry cleaning is available at a surcharge.
**Extras:** Free Wi-Fi access is available throughout the hotel and in guest rooms.

This hotel is the most expensive on Disneyland Paris property and as such its guests get some additional benefits. In addition to the standard Fastpass service available with every park entry ticket (more on this later in the guide), all guests of this hotel get one Disneyland Hotel Fastpass voucher per person per day, which allows them instant entry into one Fastpass attraction per day. This Hotel Fastpass is valid all day except between 1:00pm and 4:00pm and must be surrendered upon use.

Additionally, guests staying in the Disneyland Hotel's Castle Club or suites get one VIP Fastpass per person valid for the during of their stay. This allows unlimited entry into every Fastpass attraction at both parks without time restrictions. The Castle Club and suites also allow access into a private bar which serves complimentary non-alcohlic beverages and offers a perfect view of Disney Dreams through the windows with the music piped in.

The Celestia Spa is open from 2:00pm to 9:00pm daily. Facials are priced from €80, body treatments from €90, manicure and pedicures from €80, and full packages from €120. Reservations are recommended and can be made in person or by calling 6605 internally from the hotel room phones.

The "Club Minnie" Playroom is open from 2:00pm to 9:00pm daily and offers activities for children. The games room/arcade is open from 8:00am to 1:00am daily – children under 10 years of age must be supervised.

One fun little activity you can take part in at the hotel, whether you are staying there or not, is a silhouette portrait. For €10 you can have a side profile silhouette cut-out made of your face by an artist. You can also add a Disney character if you would like. Several price points are available going up to €40. This activity takes place in front of the boutique of the hotel and the artist is usually present five days a week (except Monday and Tuesday) from 4:00pm to 10:00pm.

**Dining:**
**Inventions** – Buffet service. Lunch is served daily from 12:30pm to 3:00pm *(Adults - €39, drinks not included; Children - €19.50 with one drink included)* and Dinner with Disney characters is served from 6:00pm to 11:00pm daily *(Adults - €54.50, drinks not included or €59.50 with one drink; Children - €29.50 with one drink included)*. Additionally, Brunch is served with the Disney Characters from 1:00pm to 3:00pm every Sunday *(Adults - €64, Children - €32)*. Selected offerings at this restaurant are included in the Premium Meal Plan and the Hotel Meal Plan.
**California Grill** – Table Service. Starters priced between €19 and €29. Main courses priced between €40 and €66. Desserts priced between €18 and €26. Set menus vary in price from €79 to €120 for adults, and are priced at €30 for children. Wines priced between €33 and €95. Disney states, "Proper attire [is] required." Open for dinner only between 6:15pm and 10:30pm. Selected offerings at this restaurant are included in the Premium Meal Plan.
**Café Fantasia** – Hotel Bar.

# Disney's Hotel New York

**Theme:** Art Deco / New York
**Transport:** Buses to the theme parks available, or a 10-minute walk through Disney Village.
**Number of rooms:** 565 rooms and 27 suites.
**Room size:** 31 square meters in standard rooms (for 4 people). Rooms in the Empire State Club level are also available including Empire State Club Rooms (can only be booked by phone) and Empire State Club Suites (including resort suites at 56 square meters, 8 honeymoon suites at 62 square meters, and 2 presidential suites measuring 166 square meters each. Suites can only be booked by phone).
**Breakfast:** Included.
**Room prices:** €236 to €435 per person per night for a standard room based on 2 adults. Empire State Club prices range from €286 to €585 per person per night.
**Activities:** Heated outdoor pool, an indoor pool, sauna and/or steam bath, tennis courts and a fitness suite. These facilities are complimentary for hotel guests. Massages are also available for an extra fee. There is also an on-site hairdresser available to both hotel and non-hotel guests. A kids' play area and a video games arcade are also available.
**Extras:** Free Wi-Fi access is available throughout the hotel and in guest rooms. This hotel houses a convention centre. Dry cleaning is available for an additional charge.

In addition to the standard Fastpass service available with every park entry ticket (more on this later in the guide), guests of this hotel staying in Empire State Club Level or in one the suites get one VIP Fastpass per person valid for the during of their stay. This allows unlimited entry into every Fastpass attraction at both parks without time restrictions.

**Dining:**
**Manhattan Restaurant** – Table Service. Main courses priced from €21 to €33. Menus priced from €36 to €56 for adults, and €30 for children. Selected offerings at this restaurant are included in the Premium Meal Plan and the Plus Meal Plan.
**Parkside Diner** – Buffet. A Breakfast Buffet (7:00am to 11:00am) is included for hotel guests but can be purchased by non-hotel guests for €12.30 for adults and €5.69 for children. Dinner buffet only (18:00 to 23:00) priced at €31 for adults without a drink, and €34.70 for adults with one drink. Children's buffets are €16. The adult buffet without a drink and the child buffet are included in the Hotel Meal Plan; the adult buffet with one drink is included in the Standard Meal Plan.
**New York City Bar** – Hotel Bar. Snacks served between 11:30am and 15:00 including sandwiches priced at €12.50 and pasta salads priced at €13.

**Top Tip:** The Hotel New York is a large hotel, which can mean that if your room is a bit further away it can be a bit of a walk in the morning when going to breakfast; you *can* request a closer room at check-in if available.

**Important**: This hotel will be closing from autumn 2015 onwards for a yearlong refurbishment. No specific dates are currently available.

# Disney's Newport Bay Club:

**Theme:** New England-Style / Nautical
**Transport:** Buses to the theme parks available, or a 15-minute walk to the parks through the Disney Village.
**Number of rooms:** 1093, including 13 suites.
**Room size:** Standard rooms measure 27 square meters (for up to 4 guests), and family rooms for up to 6 guests are also available. Suites are available varying in size (Admiral's Floor – 27 square meters, Honeymoon Suite – 50 to 63 square meters, The "Resort" Suite – 55 square meters and Presidential Suite – 84 square meters).
**Breakfast:** Included.
**Room prices:** €229 to €374 per person per night for a standard room based on 2 adults. Admiral's Floor rooms are priced at €244 to €404 per person per night.
**Activities:** An indoor pool, as well as an outdoor one with deckchairs for the warmer seasons. A complimentary sauna and/or steam bath, and a fitness suite are also available for guests of this hotel. Massages are also available for an extra charge. An indoor kids play area is also available.
**Extras:** Free Wi-Fi access is available throughout the hotel and in guest rooms. This hotel houses a convention centre. Dry cleaning is available at a surcharge.

In addition to the standard Fastpass service available with every park entry ticket (more on this later in the guide), guests of this hotel staying in Club Level or in one the suites get one VIP Fastpass per person valid for the during of their stay. This allows unlimited entry into every Fastpass attraction at both parks without time restrictions.

This hotel will be undergoing phased refurbishment until at least September 2015.

**Dining:**
**Yacht Club** – Table Service. Main courses priced between €18 and €30. Menus priced between €32 and €37 for adults and €21 for children. Selected offerings at this restaurant are included in the Premium and Plus Meal Plans.
**Cape Cod** – Buffet. Buffet menu priced at €29 for adults with no drinks included and €14 for children with one drink included. Selected offerings at this restaurant are included in the Premium and Plus Meal Plans.
**Fisherman's Wharf** – Hotel Bar.

## Disney's Sequoia Lodge:

**Theme:** American National Parks
**Transport:** Buses to the theme parks available, or a 15-minute walk to the theme parks through Disney Village.
**Number of rooms:** 1011, including 14 suites.

**Room size:** 22 square metres in a standard room. Golden Forest Club Rooms are also available, as are Honeymoon Suites and Hospitality Suites (55 square metres).
**Breakfast**: Included.
**Room prices:** €197 to €368 per person per night for a standard room based on 2 adults. Golden Forest Club rooms are priced at €227 to 428 per person per night.
**Activities:** A stunning indoor pool, as well as an outdoor section; a fitness suite; and a sauna/steam bath. Massages are also available for an extra charge. Indoor and outdoor kids play areas are also available.
**Extras:** Free Wi-Fi access is available throughout the hotel and in guest rooms. The Golden Forest Club Rooms each include a mini fridge.

In addition to the standard Fastpass service available with every park entry ticket (more on this later in the guide), guests of this hotel staying in the Golden Forest Club Level or in one the suites get one VIP Fastpass per person valid for the during of their stay. This allows unlimited entry into every Fastpass attraction at both parks without time restrictions.

Disney's Sequoia Lodge is our recommended and favourite on-site hotel. It is priced bang in the middle as far as on-site hotels are concerned but the theming and its immersive quality makes it our favourite. Make sure to take in the huge fireplace in the Redwood Bar and Lounge.

**Dining:**
**Hunter's Grill** – Buffet. Buffet menu priced at €31 without drinks or €35 with a drink for adults, and €16 with one drink for children.
**Beaver Creek Tavern** – Buffet and table service. Main courses priced between €17 and €23. Menus priced between €25 and €35 without drinks for adults, and €14 for children with one drink included.
**Redwood Bar and Lounge** – Hotel Bar and Lounge.

## Disney's Hotel Cheyenne:

**Theme:** America's Old Wild West
**Transport:** Buses to the theme parks available, or it is a 20-minute walk.
**Number of rooms:** 1000.
**Room size:** Standard rooms measure 21 square meters for up to 4 people plus 1 child under 3 years (cot upon request).
**Breakfast**: Included.
**Room prices:** €157 to €302 per person per night for a standard room based on 2 adults.
**Activities:** A video games room, as well as an outdoor and an indoor kids play area are available. Pony rides are available for an added charge. There is no pool at this hotel.
**Extras:** Free Wi-Fi available is available at the bar and in the lobby.

### Dining:
**Chuck Wagon Café** – Buffet. Continental breakfast (7:00am to 11:00am) can be purchased by non-hotel guests for €5.29 per adult and €2.39 per child. Lunch (12:30pm to 3:00pm) and dinner (6:00pm to 10:30pm) buffet – €23.50 per adult with a drink, or €27 with one drink, and €14.50 per child. The adult buffet without a drink and the child buffet are included in the Hotel Meal Plan; the adult buffet with one drink is included in Standard Meal Plan.
**Red Garter Saloon** – Hotel Bar.

# Disney's Hotel Santa Fe:

**Theme:** Southwest America (Santa Fe), and Disney Pixar's 'Cars'
**Transport:** Buses to the theme parks available, or a 20-minute walk.
**Number of rooms:** 1000.
**Room size:** A standard room measures 21 square metres (up to 4 people plus 1 child under 3 years in a cot). Family rooms for up to 6 people are also available.
**Breakfast**: Included.
**Room prices:** €157 to €302 per person per night for a standard room based on 2 adults.
**Activities:** A video game arcade is available. There is no pool at this hotel.
**Extras:** Free Wi-Fi available is available at the bar and in the lobby.

**Dining:**
**La Cantina** – Buffet. Continental breakfast can be purchased by non-hotel guests for €5.30 per adult and €2.40 per child. All day buffet – €23.50 per adult without a drink, or €27 with a drink, and €14.50 per child. The adult buffet without a drink and the child buffet are included in Hotel Meal Plan; the adult buffet with one drink is included in Standard Meal Plan.
**Rio Grande Bar** – Hotel Bar. Serves snacks priced at €6-€7 and desserts priced at €4.

29

## Disney's Davy Crockett Ranch
**Theme:** Campground
**Transport:** There are no shuttle buses available to the theme parks. It is an 8 km/15 minute drive by car to the theme parks, so you must provide your own transport.
**Number of rooms:** 595 cabins.
**Room size:** There are both 1-bedroom (36 square metres) and 2-bedroom (39 square metres) cabins available. Cabins house up to 6 people. A Premium 2-bedroom cabin option is also available.
**Breakfast**: Not included. Breakfast can be purchased for an additional charge.
**Room prices:** €122 to €302 per person per night for a standard room based on 2 adults.
**Activities:** There is a stunning heated indoor swimming pool at this resort, as well as tennis courts, a video games arcade, pony rides, quad bikes, indoor and outdoor children's play areas, a small farm and an adventure course (Davy's Crockett Adventure). Some activities require a surcharge.
**Extras:** Free Wi-Fi is available at the restaurant and the bar. The "Alamo Trading Post" grocery store sells food, clothes and souvenirs

**Dining:**
**Davy Crockett's Tavern –** Buffet. Buffet menus priced at €22 per adult and €10.50 per child.
**Crockett's Saloon –** Hotel Bar.

## Partner Hotels:
Partner hotels are not directly on the main Disneyland Paris Resort grounds but are located just outside the area, meaning they are often cheaper than Disney's own hotels. There is not much, if any, Disney theming in these hotels but they are very kid-friendly and the staff are still knowledgeable as far as shuttle bus timetables and have some knowledge of the theme parks. All these hotels provide frequent shuttle buses operated by themselves and/or Disney, and the longest shuttle bus ride is usually about 12 minutes. Most of them also have a Disney shop where in-park purchases can be delivered. Some partner hotels do not include city taxes when booked – these must be paid at check-in and are about €1 per person per night, though these can vary. Hotel meal plans are not valid at these hotels' restaurants.

The partner hotels include the Radisson Blu Hotel, Vienna Magic Circus, Vienna Dream Castle Hotel, Alongquin's Explorers Hotel, L'Elysee Val d' Europe, Adagio City Aparthotel and the Kyriad.

## Radisson Blu Hotel
**Transport:** Free shuttle service to the theme parks.
**Number of rooms:** 250 guest rooms and suites.
**Room size:** Standard room (30 square metres, maximum occupancy: 2 adults and 1 child aged under 3), Family room (30 square metres, maximum occupancy: up to 4 adults), Junior Suite (60 square metres), Suite (70 square metres) and Presidential Suite (90 square metres).
**Breakfast**: Included in most rates.
**Room prices:** Sample price per person per night (based on 2 adults per room): €195
**Activities:** Swimming pool, fitness centre, spa, and an outdoor play area. The hotel is also located on the Disneyland Paris golf course, with 9 and 18-hole courses available to play on (additional charges apply).
**Extras:** Free Wi-Fi is available throughout the hotel, including in guest rooms. Meeting rooms are available at this hotel.

**Dining**:
Pamplemousse – French table service cuisine
Birdie – Buffet.
Le Chardon - Bar.

## Vienna International Dream Castle Hotel
**Transport:** Free shuttle service to the theme parks.
**Number of rooms:** 397 rooms and suites.
**Room size:** Double rooms and family rooms (28 square metres), double queen rooms (44 square metres), Rapunzel suite (54 square metres), The Baron von Münchhausen Suite (60 square metres) and The Royal Suite (220 square metres).
**Breakfast**: Included in most rates.
**Room prices:** Sample price per person per night (based on 2 adults per room): €154
**Activities:** Swimming pool, fitness centre, spa, indoor and outdoor play area, carousel, and a video game room.
**Extras:** Free Wi-Fi is available throughout the hotel, including in guest rooms.

**Dining**:
Les Trois Mosquetaires – Buffet
Excalibur – Bar.


## Vienna International Magic Circus Hotel
**Transport:** Free shuttle service to the theme parks.
**Number of rooms:** 396 rooms and suites.
**Room size:** Double rooms and family rooms (28 square metres), and suites (up to 60 square metres).
**Breakfast**: Included in most rates.
**Room prices:** Sample price per person per night (based on 2 adults per room): €154
**Activities:** Swimming pool and fitness centre.
**Extras:** Free Wi-Fi is available throughout the hotel, including in guest rooms.

**Dining:**
L'Etoile – Buffet
Bar des Artistes – Bar

## Adagio ApartHotel Marne la Vallee / Val d'Europe
**Transport:** Free shuttle service to the theme parks.
**Number of rooms:** 290 studios and apartments.
**Room size:** Studios (21 square metres), 1 bedroom (27 square metres to 40 square metres) and 2 to 3 bedroom apartments (27 square metres to 53 square metres)
**Breakfast**: Included in most rates in the breakfast room.
**Room prices:** Sample price per person per night (based on 2 adults per room): €147
**Activities:** Swimming pool
**Extras:** Free Wi-Fi is available throughout the hotel, including in guest rooms. There is no on-site restaurant (except for the buffet breakfast). Rooms include a kitchenette to plan and cook your own meals.

## Alongquin's Explorers Hotel
**Transport:** Free shuttle service to the theme parks.
**Number of rooms:** 390.
**Room size:** Standard crew rooms measure 18 to 22 square metres. Other room sizes vary.
**Breakfast**: Included in most rates.
**Room prices:** Sample price per person per night (based on 2 adults per room): €139
**Activities:** Swimming pool, indoor and outdoor play areas, video games room, and kids fitness area.
**Extras:** Free Wi-Fi is available throughout the hotel, including in guest rooms. Themed suites are also available including Planet Hollywood, Sweet and Jungle themes.

**Dining**:
**La Plantation** – Buffet
**Captain's Library** – Table Service

**Marco's Pizza** – Quick Service
**The Traders** – Bar

## Hotel l'Elysee (Val d'Europe)
**Transport:** Free shuttle service to the theme parks.
**Number of rooms:** 152 rooms, including 4 executive suites.
**Room size:** Cosy rooms (24 square metres for up to 2 people), family rooms (24 square metres for up to 4 people), family XL rooms (up to 48 square metres for up to 8 people), and executive suites (38 square metres for up to 4 people).
**Breakfast:** Included in most rates.
**Room prices:** Sample price per person per night (based on 2 adults per room): €136
**Activities:** No extra amenities.
**Extras:** Free Wi-Fi is available throughout the hotel, including in guest rooms. Meeting rooms are available. Laundry can be done for an additional charge.

**Dining:**
**Restaurant** – Table service (lunch only).
**L'Etoile** – Bar.

## Kyriad Hotel
**Transport:** Free shuttle service to the theme parks.
**Number of rooms:** 300.
**Room size:** Standard rooms measure 18.5 square metres, and accommodate between 2 and 4 people.
**Breakfast:** Included in most rates.
**Room prices:** Sample price per person per night (based on 2 adults per room): €149
**Activities:** Carousel, video games room, and indoor children's play area.
**Extras:** Free Wi-Fi is available throughout the hotel, including in guest rooms.
**Dining:**
Le Marché Gourmand – Buffet
L'Abreuvoir – Bar

Partner hotels may be booked through the Disneyland Paris reservation phone line or website where park tickets will be included in the total price – these can be retrieved at check-in time. Partner hotels can also be booked directly on their own websites or through third-party websites and travel agents, in most cases park tickets will not be included in these rates.

## Easy Pass:

The Easy Pass is exclusive to the seven Disneyland Paris operated hotels, and is given to guests upon check-in. The Easy Pass allows you entry into Disneyland Park during Extra Magic Hours. The card is also used for access to the swimming pools in the hotels, and for free parking both at the hotel and at the main Disneyland theme park parking lot.

During check-in you can also link a credit or debit card to your Easy Pass which will allow you to pay for food and merchandise at most resort locations using the Easy Pass instead of paying with your own card or in cash each time. You then settle the bill when checking out and pay one lump sum. This can be a particularly cost effective option for people who do not live in France whose credit card companies may charge a per-transaction fee. Just be sure to monitor your spending so as to not go over budget.

Note: Some small stalls (such as those selling drink or popcorn) do not accept the Easy Pass; this also applies to non-Disney operated restaurants in Disney Village.

## Where/how to book partner and non-Disney hotels:

There are many different ways to book non-Disney and partner hotels. These include travel agents, directly on a hotel's website and through a booking aggregator.

Personally, we have always booked partner hotels through a booking aggregator called Hotels.com – use our link http://www.independentguidebooks.com/bookhotels. This website is generally well priced but also has a money-back guarantee in case you do find the hotel cheaper elsewhere. Also, it often offers cancellations up to 24 hours before check-in. In addition, you can collect Hotels.com reward nights if you sign up to the "Welcome Rewards" program, which includes over 100,000 hotels worldwide.

Be sure to also check out the following two sites for the best rates:
- Booking.com which also offers attractive rates – our link for that is www.independentguidebooks.com/bookinghotels
- Priceline.com which allows you to book hotels in the usual manner, or to specify how much you want to pay – our link is www.independentguidebooks.com/priceline

Of course you are not limited to Disneyland Paris' partner hotels. There are many hotels that have not partnered with Disneyland Paris but are located nearby. For example, if you are on a budget and want a basic apart-hotel, you could try "Sejours et Affairs" in Val d'Europe.

## Official Disney Hotel special offers and making changes:

The cheapest place to book Disneyland Paris hotels or packages is through the official website at www.independentguidebooks.com/bookdlp (or www.disneylandparis.com) The website offers you several room types but unfortunately suites cannot be booked online, and must be booked over the phone. Both the Disneyland Paris website and phone reservations currently charge a £16 booking fee. Travel agents may also feature special rates.

Disneyland Paris regularly runs promotions allowing you to save anywhere between 10-50% off the price, or get free nights when you book a stay. If there is not a sale when you are thinking of booking, we would not recommend booking as there will most likely be a sale just a few days away.

Sales and offers vary seasonally and between different countries. These can include anything from 'free hotel and park tickets for under 7s', to 'free hotel, park tickets and transport for under 12s', 'free half board meal plans', and even up to 40% or even 50% off. A minimum stay of two or three nights usually applies to these promotions, as well as date restrictions.

**Top Tip 1:** Remember that you can also book Disneyland Paris (and partner) hotels over the phone, which gives you one more advantage; you can pay in installments instead of one lump sum (there is no extra interest if you decide to choose this option). This means that you are able to modify your booking until you have paid the full amount. Therefore, if a better offer becomes available after you have made your booking, you will be able to make changes such as upgrading your hotel or adding extra meal vouchers easily.

**Top Tip 2:** Disneyland Paris often runs different promotions in different areas of Europe. For example the resort can simultaneously run a 20% off promotion in the UK and 40% off in Belgium. The good news is you can actually book any of the promotions available in any country. Simply visit [www.disneylandparis.com](www.disneylandparis.com) - at the bottom of the page click 'change your country' and select another country and then try booking through there. Note you will have to pay in the currency local to that country which you can do with any credit or debit card, although some banks do charge fees for doing this. Please note that the language of the website may also change when you do this. You are also able to do this by calling up Disneyland Paris directly and stating the offer you would like to take advantage of.

Here is an example of the different promotions available in different regions that were available at the time of writing this guide. The UK Disneyland Paris website offered 30% off stays, the German website offered a 200 euro discount off stays, the Italian website offered 20% off stays, the US website offered 1 day and night free, and the Spanish website offered 15% off stays and with free meals. Clearly, there are all very different offers with different savings depending on your needs.

Chapter 6
# Tickets

There are many ways of buying entry tickets for Disneyland Paris. These range from vouchers, to annual passports, buying tickets at the gates, online, at a Disney Store and more. Prices, special offers and ticket lengths vary between these different methods. To help you decide which is the best option for you, here is a detailed look at Disneyland Paris' tickets.

**Top Tip:** If you have booked a Disney hotel through the Disneyland Paris booking website or over the phone then you can skip this section, as your tickets are included in your package price unless you specifically asked for them not to be.

## Buying Tickets At The Park Gates:
For guests who turn up to Disneyland Paris spontaneously, it is possible to purchase tickets at the ticket booths located at the entrance of each theme park. However, as you have purchased this guide, we can rule this out. You are prepared and know you will be visiting the resort so there is no reason to purchase the tickets at the rime of arrival. 'Gate prices' (purchased on-site at Disneyland Paris) are the most expensive and you can get a substantial discount by booking in advance, and save a lot of time.

## Gate prices:
**1 day/1 park -** Adults: €75; Children €67
**1 day/2 parks -** Adults: €90; Children €82
**2 days/2 parks -** Adults: €139; Children €126
**3 days/2 parks -** Adults: €174; Children €158
**4 days/2 parks -** Adults: €209; Children €190
**5 days/2 parks -** Adults: €229; Children €211 (5-day ticket price not publicly displayed)

NB: Children are classed as 3 to 11 year olds. Children under 3 years of age enter for free – proof of age may be requested. Ticket prices last increased on 1$^{st}$ May 2015.

The ticket booths for Disneyland Park are located under the pink Disneyland Hotel on the way in to the park. Ticket booths for the Walt Disney Studios Park are located to the right of the entrance turnstiles of the park. You are able to purchase one-park or two-park tickets for one or multiple days at any of the ticket booths.

In 2014, Disneyland Paris also introduced automated ticket booths under the Disneyland Hotel, which are another option.

## Online:
If you purchase your tickets in advance online you can make significant savings on the standard 'gate' prices. The price of your ticket will vary based on the date of your visit and its length.

**1-Day tickets:**
**Billet Mini**
- 1 day/1 park – Adults: £39/€47; Children: £33/€40
- 1 day/2 parks – Adults: £51/€62; Children: £45/€55

**Billet Magic**
- 1 day/1 park – Adults: £49/€59; Children: £43/€52
- 1 day/2 parks – Adults: £61/€74; Children: £55/€67

**Super Magic Ticket**
- 1 day/1 park - Adults: £57/€69; Children: £51/€62
- 1 day/2 parks - Adults: £69/€84; Children £64/€77

Certain tickets are valid only on certain dates. The Super Magic ticket is valid every day of the year. Specific dates can be seen using the grid below:

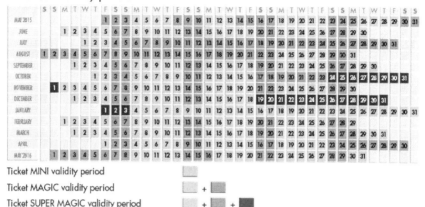

Online pre-purchased one-day tickets can be booked up to one day prior to the date of your visit and are valid for 1 year from the day following the date of purchase. They can be used on any day of the year except for the day of purchase itself. If you opt to have the tickets posted to your home address (additional charges will apply), the tickets must be booked at least 10 days prior to the date of your visit. E-tickets can be booked up to one day prior to the date of your visit.

**Multi-day tickets:**
The following prices are for standard multi-day tickets bought in advance via the Disneyland Paris website:
- 2 days/2 parks – Adults: £115/€139 Children: £104/€126
- 3 days/2 parks – Adults: £144/€169 Children: £131/€156
- 4 days/2 parks – Adults: £173/€209 Children: £157/€189

There are also two special offer tickets available online but make sure to read the terms and conditions as these vary from the standard multi-day tickets above:
- 4 days/2 parks – Adults £144/Children £131. Pay for 3 days and get an extra day free.
- 5 days/2 parks – Adults £173/Children £157. Pay for 4 days and get an extra day free.

You can purchase tickets online via our direct link to the official Disneyland Paris website at
www.independentguidebooks.com/dlptickets

**Ticket Brokers:**
There are also several ticket brokers out there that provide genuine discounted attraction tickets, sometimes with huge savings! Here are some our favourite and most trusted ones. Be sure to check them all out for the best prices:
- Attraction Tickets Direct – www.independentguidebooks.com/atd
- AttractionTix – www.independentguidebooks.com/attractiontix
- 365Tickets - http://www.365tickets.co.uk/disneyland-paris

**Top Tip:** For a non-promotional multi-day ticket (2 days or longer) you do not have to use the days consecutively, but merely within 1 year of the purchase date. So you could use 2 days of a 5-day ticket in summer and then the remaining 3 days at Christmas for example. Be sure to check you ticket conditions before booking.

**Vouchers:**
If you are a member of UK collection points scheme Avios (formerly Airmiles), you can gain entry into the Disneyland Paris theme parks using 8500 Avios for a 1 Day/2-Park adult ticket (ages 12 and over) and 7500 Avios for a 1 Day/2-Park child ticket (ages 3 to 11). Call Avios to exchange your points for park tickets or you can also do it through the Avios website. These are actual tickets, which allow you entry straight through the turnstiles without having to exchange them. Multi-day tickets are also available if you call Avios, but are not available online.

# Disney Stores:

You can buy tickets at any Disney Store in the UK for Disneyland Paris and most Disney Stores around Europe. Tickets for Disneyland Paris may also be stocked at selected other Disney Stores worldwide. Just ask at the counter. These tickets are priced at theme park ticket booth rates, but will save you time queuing when at the resort. If you are going to be buying in advance then we recommend you do so online in order to get the best savings.

## Ticket Tips:

- 2-park tickets are often called "Park Hoppers" as they allow you to go from one park to the other park as many times as you want throughout the same day.
- When leaving either park, ask to have your hand stamped to allow re-entry (this system is not in operation every day).
- You will need at least one day to tour the Walt Disney Studios Park comfortably and a minimum of two days to tour the Disneyland Park comfortably. It is equally easy to spend four or five days at the resort taking in the experiences on offer at a more leisurely pace.
- If you are visiting for three day or longer consider getting an Annual Passport, which allows you into the parks up to 365 days a year. Additionally, the Annual Passport provides some great discounts on food, hotels, merchandise and other experiences.
- Student tickets (for students aged 18 to 25 with valid proof) and Senior tickets (for those aged over 60 with valid proof) are available at the ticket booths at the parks. The large family ticket for families with at least 3 children is also available solely at the park entry ticket booths.

## Annual Passports:

Buying a Disneyland Paris *Passeport Annuel* is easy and gives you a whole year of benefits for the price of just a few days' admission. Your *Passeport* includes discounts and entry into the park. Annual passes are available to anyone regardless of their country.

Pricing is valid until 2$^{nd}$ November 2015 inclusive.

| Passeport Annuel Francilien - €135 | Passeport Annuel Fantasy - €179 | Passeport Annuel Dream - €223 |
|---|---|---|
| Access to the parks 280 days per year. Cannot be used the two days following activation. | Access to the parks 320 days per year. | Access to the parks 365 days per year. |
| 10% discount on Christmas and Halloween special events. | 20% discount on Christmas and Halloween special events. | 30% discount on Christmas and Halloween special events. |
| Unlimited parking can be purchased for an additional €30. | Unlimited parking is included. | Unlimited parking is included. |
| 10% discount in shops. | 10% discount in shops. | 20% discount in shops. |
| 10% discount at restaurants | 10% discount at restaurants | 10% discount at restaurants |
| Up to 25% off Disney hotel room-only bookings | Up to 25% off Disney hotel room-only bookings | Up to 35% off Disney hotel room-only bookings |
|  | 20% off Buffalo Bills Wild West Dinner Show | 20% off Buffalo Bills Wild West Dinner Show |
|  | 10% off 1 day park entry tickets for friends and family | 20% off 1 day park entry tickets for friends and family |
|  | Access to Extra Magic Hours on non-blockout days | Access to all Extra Magic Hours |

In addition, Dream Annual Passport holders also get:
- Invitations to special events
- A free non-alcoholic starter in table service restaurants
- Free stroller/wheelchair rentals, lockers, as well as kennel facilities for animals.
- 10% off at Disneyland Paris Golf
- 10% off all Disney stores in France.
- 30% off cinema tickets in the Disney Village Gaumont Cinema. (This applies to all annual passport holders)
- 15% off Davy Crockett Adventure (This applies to all annual passport holders)

Students can get fantastic value by purchasing a "Passeport Annuel Etudiant" for only €89. It offers the same benefits as a Francilien passport with 280 days of entry per year. Students must present a photo ID and valid student ID (ages 18 to 25) when purchasing the passport.

**How do I get my annual passport?**
At the park entrance ticket booths ask whether they can do an annual pass there and then - this is often available on quieter days of the week, and some weekends. Alternatively, ask if "Donald's Desk" is open today, if so follow the Cast Member's directions and complete the passport at Donald's Desk.

If the desk is not open, the process is simple: you buy a one-day ticket to go into Disneyland Park (not Walt Disney Studios Park). Once inside Disneyland Park ask a Cast Member for the "Bureau Passport Annuel" (located at the entrance of Discoveryland). Here you will be asked for some details such as your address and name, have a photo taken for the card and get your annual passport to take with you. The price of your day ticket will be deducted from your annual passport's price. Allow about an hour for this as there may be a queue of people - the actual process itself takes less than 10 minutes. Have a passport or ID card with you as proof of identity.

**What are the blackout dates? (The dates the annual pass cannot be used)**

|  | **Passeport Annuel Francilien (280 days of access per year)** | **Passeport Annuel Fantasy (320 days of access per year)** |
|---|---|---|
| January 2015 | 1st, 6th, 13th, 20th and 27th | 1st, 6th, 13th, 20th and 27th |
| February 2015 | 3rd | None |
| March 2015 | 21st, 22nd, 28th and 29th | 28th and 29th |
| April 2015 | 4th and 5th | 4th and 5th |
| May 2015 | 2nd, 9th, 16th, 24th and 30th | 16th and 24th |
| June 2015 | 2nd, 9th, 16th, 20th, 23rd, 27th and 28th | 2nd, 9th, 16th, 27th and 28th |
| July 2015 | 4th, 5th, 7th, 8th, 9th and 10th | 4th only |
| August 2015 | 22nd, 29th and 30th | 29th only |
| September 2015 | 1st, 8th, 12th, 15th, 19th, 20th, 22nd, 26th, 27th and 29th | 1st, 8th, 15th, 22nd, 26th and 27th |
| October 2015 | 6th, 13th, 20th, 24th, 25th, 26th, 27th, 28th, 29th, 30th and 31st | 6th, 13th, 20th, 24th, 25th and 31st |
| November 2015 | 1st, 2nd, 3rd, 7th, 8th, 14th, 17th, 21st, 24th, 28th and 29th | 1st, 7th, 14th, 17th and 28th |
| December 2015 | 1st, 5th, 6th, 8th, 12th, 13th, 19th, 20th, 26th, 27th, 28th, 29th, 30th and 31st | 15th, 19th and 26th |

The **Dream Annual Passport** can be used every day of the year with no blackout dates.

The blackout dates do not apply to the date you buy your annual passport, meaning that you can use it for entry on the day you buy the annual pass even if it is a blackout day – you will however not be able to park-hop during that day.

There is a 20% family discount if buying five Fantasy or Dream annual passes together.

**Chapter 7**
# Disneyland Park

Disneyland Park, dubbed 'Parc Disneyland' in French, is based on the original Disneyland opened in California back in 1955. Every Disney resort around the world has one of these classic "Magic Kingdom-Style" Disney parks, and this is the largest spanning 140 acres.

Disneyland Park is the most visited theme park in Europe and the sixth most visited in the world with 10.4 million visitors last year. The park has plenty on offer with almost fifty attractions (rides, themed areas and shows), as well as character experiences and more. This park is easily the most beautiful theme park in Europe in our opinion, and it has been dubbed the most beautiful Disney theme park in the world.

The park is divided into five areas (or "lands") around Sleeping Beauty Castle in the centre. Around the edges of the park, you will find the Disneyland Railroad, which transports guests between these different lands.

In this section, in order to help you determine how long you may wait to experience attractions there are "average wait times" quoted; these are for peak times such as school holidays (Summer, Christmas, Easter) and weekends throughout the whole year.

# Main Street U.S.A:

As you enter the park you will be 'walking right down the middle of Main Street U.S.A,' as you head towards the hub of the park, Sleeping Beauty castle, and beyond. Equally you will end your day by walking down the street. Main Street U.S.A. has shops on both sides of the road - the king of which is the Emporium where you are sure to find something to buy! There are places to eat up and down the street too including quick service and table service restaurants, as well as snack locations.

**Top Tip:** Running parallel to Main Street U.S.A. on its left and right are the Liberty Arcade and the Discovery Arcade, which provide an alternative route for when it is raining.

City Hall is immediately to your left on Town Square before entering the street itself, this is essentially "guest services" - any questions you have can be answered here, they can make reservations, and accept complaints and congratulations too. For disabled guests, an accessibility card is available here too providing easier access to attractions. See our guests with disabilities chapter for more information on this.

Main Street U.S.A. houses several attractions including **Dapper Dan's Hair Cuts** (a real barbershop, reservation recommended); **Horse-Drawn Streetcars**, **Main Street Vehicles**, and the **Main Street U.S.A.'s Railroad Station**.

Notable restaurants include:

**Walt's Restaurant** – Table service restaurant. The *Formule Menu Carte* set menu is priced at €30 for a two course meal, or €36 for a three course meal. A three course *Menu Grand Classique* set menu is also available priced at €43. Drinks are not included in adult set menus. Mains ordered a la carte are priced between €26 and €33. The *Menu Enfant* is available for children up to 11 years old inclusive, and is priced at €16. The €36 *Formule Menu Carte* and *Menu Enfant* are included in the Plus Meal Plan. A la carte menu items can also be ordered as part of the Premium Meal Plan.

**Casey's Corner** – Counter service restaurant serving ballgame themed snacks. Classic hot dogs – €7; 8-piece chicken nuggets – €7.70; salad - €7; desserts - €3 to €4; hot and cold drinks €2.70 to €3.30; teatime treat - €5.50; beer - €5.30). Cheddar and onions can be added for a few cents more to the hot dogs.

**Plaza Gardens** – Buffet restaurant. Adult buffet priced at €29.50 with unlimited drinks or €25.50 without drinks. Child buffet priced at €16 with one drink. Both adult and children menus with drinks are included in the Standard Meal Plan.

**Victoria's Home-Style Restaurant** – Counter Service restaurant. Hot sandwiches - €7; side salad - €3.50; crisps - €2.30; desserts - €3 to €4; hot and cold drinks €2.70 to €3.30; teatime treat - €5.50; beer - €5.30

There are also other little food shops and carts around Main Street too. For shopping, the biggest store here is **Emporium**, but there are also many other stores to choose from.

**Top Tip:** Throughout the day at unannounced times the fountains located in the moat of Sleeping Beauty Castle will come to life along with music for special two to three minute happenings. This takes place eight times per day but no schedule is officially published – if you are there on the hour or at half past the hour you are more likely to see these. These fountain shows change according to the seasons. For example there are unique fountain shows during Halloween and St. Patrick's Day.

## Attractions
### Disneyland Railroad – Main Street Station
Take a grand tour of Disneyland Park on boar an authentic steam train. Whether you use it as a form of transport or just a way of seeing the sights, the railroad is a fun way to look at the park. A round tour of the park takes approximately 30 minutes. This attraction will usually cease operation several hours before the park closes.

### Main Street Vehicles and Horse-Drawn Streetcars
What better way to see Main Street than from a vehicle – whether it is a horsedrawn car, a double decker bus or one of the other forms of transport. These vehicles only operate in the morning hours until approximately midday.

# Frontierland:
Step into Frontierland and be transported to the Wild West of the United States and the town of Thunder Mesa.

### Attractions:
The main attractions here are: **Big Thunder Mountain, Phantom Manor** and **Thunder Mesa Riverboat Landing**.

Other attractions in this land include the **Frontierland Railroad Station,** the **Keelboats** which have been closed for several years, the **Chaparral Theatre** stage (currently there are no permanent shows playing at this location) and a Pocahontas themed outdoor playground.

There is also the **Rustler Roundup Shootin' Gallery** where you can practice your shooting skills by trying to hit several targets in a carnival-style game. This is an additional charge for this attraction.

# Big Thunder Mountain:

**Fastpass**: Yes
**Minimum Height**: 1.02m
**On-ride photo**: Yes
**Ride length**: 4 minutes
**Average wait times**: 90 to 120 minutes
**Loading**: 2400 people per hour

Jump aboard a family rollercoaster sure to bring a smile to everyone's face. The story goes that in the late 1800s the town of Thunder Mesa where Big Thunder Mountain is located was discovered, and a line of trains was constructed to transport the ore around the mountain. Little did the residents know that the town was cursed and it was subsequently struck by an earthquake. Residents left the town, and a few years later the trains were found driving themselves around the mountain. Guests are now allowed to experience a ride in one of these mine carts for themselves.

This ride is quite long lasting around four minutes, which is unusual for a rollercoaster. Along the way you will see collapsing bridges, dynamite, bats and more on this wild, wild ride! Most of the action takes place on an island in the middle of the lake, making it a totally unique version of the ride when compared to other Disney parks. It is also the longest, tallest and fastest of any of the Big Thunder Mountain rides around the world. At the end, you can also collect your on-ride photo for an extra charge. Smile for the camera!

This is definitely one of our favourite attractions in the whole park and one that can usually be experienced by the whole family.

## Phantom Manor:

**Fastpass**: No
**Minimum Height**: None
**On-ride photo**: No
**Ride length**: 7 minutes
**Average wait times**: Up to 30 mins
**Loading**: 2 guests per doombuggy, 131 doombuggies - 2100 guests per hour.

This ride is sure to get the whole family excited as you venture through the derelict manor. The story is based on Melanie, a bride featured in the ride, who on her wedding day eagerly awaited her groom, while a phantom came to haunt the house. The phantom lured the groom into the attic and hung him. Melanie waited for her groom but he never turned up. Now, she roams around the manor still in her wedding dress looking for new friends.

The ride is definitely a must see: the atmosphere, music and details are some of the best in the resort. Be aware that there are some loud noises at the beginning, which may frighten some younger children.

The audio at the beginning of the attraction is solely in French, which can make the attraction more difficult to understand for some visitors. The attraction is part-walkthrough and part-ride. Guests ride in "doombuggies" that rotate and tilt to show you the mansion as you venture through it.

There are no jump-out scares but the loud laughter during the walkthrough section may frighten some children as can some of the animatronics in the 'cemetery' scene. It is in no way a horror-maze type attraction and because it has no height restrictions, the attraction is accessible to all ages. Though do be wary of younger kids.

The storyline of this attraction is completely unique, despite similar rides existing at other Disney parks worldwide. Ride it!

## Thunder Mesa Riverboat Landing:

**Fastpass**: No
**Minimum Height**: None
**On-ride photo**: No
**Ride length**: 15 minutes
**Average wait times**: Less than 30 mins – until the next boat
**Loading**: Each boat carries 390 passengers, 1 boat with load time - 800 guests per hour.

Set sail on a classic riverboat around Big Thunder Mountain and admire the stunning landscape of Frontierland. The Thunder Mesa Riverboat is a nice, relaxing change from the usual crowds of the park with space to roam around the ship. There are some (limited) seating areas and you can hear the story of the Molly Brown as you go around the river via the speakers.

**Top Tip:** Opening times for the Riverboat are shorter than for most other attractions. The riverboat usually opens one hour after park opening and ceases operation in the middle of the afternoon.

## Dining:
Places to eat here include:

**Silver Spur Steakhouse** – Table service restaurant. Three-course *Menu du Sherif* set menu priced at €30 and three-course *Menu du Cowboy* set menu priced at €36 for adults. No drinks are included in adult menus. Main courses priced between €17.50 and €27.50 if ordered a la carte. Children's set menu priced at €16 with one drink included. Children's set menu and Menu du Cowboy are both included in the Plus Meal Plan.

**The Lucky Nugget Saloon** – Counter service restaurant. Menus priced at €14 to €16 for an adult, and €8 for a child.

**Cowboy Cookout BBQ** – Quick service restaurant. Menus priced at €12 to €15 for adults and €8 for children.

**Fuente del Oro** – Counter service restaurant serving Mexican fare. Menus priced at €12 to €15. Children's menu priced at €8.50.

**Last Chance Cafe** – Counter service restaurant. Take-away snack-type meals priced at €7 to €11. Desserts, beer and hot and cold drinks are also available at this location.

# Adventureland:

Venture into an Arabian story, into the Caribbean or into a temple with Indiana Jones – all in the most exotic of lands.

## Attractions:
The main attractions here are: **Pirates of the Caribbean, Indiana Jones et le Temple du Peril, Adventure Isle** (a walk through area that features winding paths, a series of caves, a pirate ship and a suspension bridges), **La Cabane des Robinsons** (walk-through), **Le Passage Enchante d'Aladdin** (a walkthrough attraction depicting scenes from the story of Aladdin) and **La Plage des Pirates** (an outdoor playground).

## Indiana Jones et le Temple du Peril:

**Fastpass**: Yes
**Minimum Height:** 1.40m
**On-ride photo:** No
**Ride length:** 2 minute 10 seconds
**Average wait times:** 30 to 60 minutes
**Loading:** 2 guests per row, 12 per train. Up to 1400 guests an hour.

This ride will take you on an archeological adventure through the lost Temple of Doom.

Your adventure will have you climbing in search of treasure, dropping, going around tight corners and meandering in and around the Temple – even including a 360-degree loop.

This is one of the most intense coasters at the resort with the loop being particularly tight. Other than that, it is relatively short but a fun experience.

The ride has the biggest minimum-height limit of any ride at any Disney park worldwide – 140cm. It was also the first Disney rollercoaster in the world to go upside down. The ride ran backwards for a few years but now runs forward once again.

**Top Tip**: When park attendance is low, Fastpass is not offered at this attraction.

## Pirates of the Caribbean:

**Fastpass:** No
**Minimum Height:** None
**On-ride photo:** Yes
**Ride length:** 10 minutes
**Average wait times:** 15 to 45 minutes. You can generally walk-on at less busy times.
**Loading:** 23 guests per boat, 24 boats. Approximately 3000 guests per hour.

Ahoy me hearties! Set sail through the world of the Pirates of the Caribbean at Disneyland Paris. This attraction is based on the original ride as it was installed in Disneyland in California. Pirates of the Carribean was the final ride Walt Disney himself supervised the creation of.

This version of the attraction is the only version of the ride in the world *not* to feature the characters from the famous "Pirates of the Caribbean" blockbusters. However, there are rumours that Jack Sparrow may soon find himself into the ride.

Disneyland Paris' version of the ride is in our opinion the best version of all the Pirates rides with the most coherent storyline, elaborate theming, stunning sets, and biggest drops.

Guests board boats that take them on a ten-minute journey into a pirate world. There are flume drops and the audio-animatronic characters in the attraction are enthralling. The technology has evolved greatly since the first Pirates ride was installed, meaning that guests at Disneyland Paris see the most advanced and realistic characters of their kind.

Be aware that the queue line for the ride is not well lit due to the atmosphere it aims to create and therefore it is very, very dark. This will especially strike you during the daytime when your eyes take a while to adjust, so we would advise holding onto your children's hands throughout the queue.

This ride loads guests onto the boats in an extremely efficient manner meaning that there are very rarely queues of above 20 minutes, and many times you will be on the ride under 10 minutes, except during the very busiest of times. This is undoubtedly one of the best-themed attractions in the world and is a family friendly, must-see ride.

## Dining:
**Blue Lagoon** – Table service restaurant. Adult set menus priced between €29 and €40. Children's set menu priced at €15.

**Agrabah Cafe** – Buffet restaurant. The adult buffet is priced at €25.50 without drinks or €29 with one drink included. The children's buffet is priced at €16 with one drink included. Both the child buffet and the adult buffet with drink are included in the Standard Meal Plan.
**Colonel Hathi's Pizza Outpost** – Counter Service restaurant. Menus priced between €12 and €15. Children's menu priced at €8.50.
**Hakuna Matata** – Counter Service restaurant. Menus priced at €11 to €14. Children's menu priced at €8.
**Coolpost** – Snack location. Teatime snack with drink and crepe - €5.50; ice creams - €3 to €4; and crepes €3 to €4. Other small snacks, as well as hot and cold drinks are also available.

## Characters:
You can often find **Captain Jack Sparrow** roaming around meeting guests outside the entrance to Blue Lagoon Restaurant and the exit to Pirates of the Caribbean. The daily park schedule will usually feature times for this meet-and-greet.

# Fantasyland:

Find classic Disney attractions here, in this land dedicated to the littlest ones in the family.

## Attractions:

The gentle toddler-friendly rides are all here in the most magical of all the lands, and there is a lot of variety: **Sleeping Beauty Castle** which houses **The Dragon's Lair** (La Taniere du Dragon) and **Sleeping Beauty's Gallery** (La Galerie de la Belle au Bois Dormant) are both great detailed walk-through attractions, and both inside the castle. The Dragon's Lair contains a huge animatronic dragon that can potentially be frightening for children, and even some adults.

Other rides include **it's a small world, Peter Pan's Flight, Snow White and the Seven Dwarfs** (Blanche-Neige et les Sept Nains), **The Adventures of Pinocchio** (Les Voyages de Pinocchio), **Dumbo, Lancelot's Carrousel, Mad Hatter's Tea Cups, Alice's Curious Labyrinth, Storybook Land** (Le Pays des Contes de Fees), **Casey Jr., Fantasyland Disneyland Railroad Station.** As far as entertainment and character meets are concerned there is **Meet Mickey Mouse, Princess Pavilion** and the **Castle Stage** (Le Theatre du Chateau – currently no permanent show is scheduled for this stage).

**Top Tip**: Fantasyland closes one hour earlier than the rest of the park to clear the area when fireworks are performed (daily until further notice).

## Peter Pan's Flight:

**Fastpass:** Yes
**Minimum Height:** None
**On-ride photo**: No
**Ride length**: 3 minutes
**Average wait times**: 90 to 120 minutes
**Loading**: Up to 6 guests per flying pirate ship, 16 ships - 1500 guests per hour.

Peter Pan's Flight is one of Disneyland Paris' most popular rides – it features popular characters, it is family friendly and provides a bit of a thrill too. Hop aboard a flying pirate ship and take a voyage through the world of Peter Pan and Never Never Land.
As you soar you will see scenes unfold besides you and beneath you too, retelling the classic story of Peter Pan. The interior to this ride is stunning from the moment you step in and truly immersive.

This is an incredibly popular ride so using a Fastpass is recommended to avoid a long wait. Alternatively, visit the attraction in the morning, in the evening or during the parade. On busy days the Fastpasses for this ride will run out by around lunchtime.

**Important Note**: Visitors who are afraid of heights may find this ride unsuitable. The flying ships you travel in really do give the sensation of flight and at times you will be several metres off the ground and descending steeply (albeit not too quickly). At other times the rail above will almost disappear and you will appear to be really flying. These sensations may surprise some guests – mostly though it seems to be adults who are affected by this, and not children.

## Alice's Curious Labyrinth:

**Fastpass:** No
**Minimum Height:** None
**Attraction length**: Between 10 and 20 minutes
**Average wait times**: Under 5 minutes
**Loading**: Walk-through maze.

Ever fancied getting *lost* in the world of Alice in Wonderland? Well now you can literally do exactly that! This maze has a good variation of elements and is just challenging enough to keep you guessing where to go next. There are quite a few photo opportunities along the way too. Once you reach the end of the maze you have the option of returning back to the park, or climbing the Queen's castle instead. This is worth doing for a stunning view over the park. The labyrinth is good family fun and a good way for the little ones to burn some energy.

# it's a small world:

**Fastpass**: No
**Minimum Height**: None
**On-ride photo**: No
**Ride length**: 10 minutes and 30 seconds
**Average wait times**: Under 20 minutes
**Loading**: 23 riders per boat, 24 boats. About 2400 guests per hour.

'It's a small world' is of the most resort's most memorable and popular attractions, featuring hundreds of dolls singing a tune about the uniting of the world. You can guarantee you will remember the lyrics.

Guests board a boat and travel leisurely through scenes depicting different countries from around the world, as the attraction's song is recited in different languages.

The loading system is incredibly efficient on this ride meaning that the number of people who can enjoy the ride every hour is high – for you, this means that queues are often very short.

This ride is a great Disney classic that, although not based on any film franchise, is one of the many "must-dos" for many visitors.

Fun fact: This ride has more audio-animatronics that any other attraction in the park.

## Princess Pavilion:
**Fastpass**: No (but reservations are required at certain times of the year)
**Minimum Height**: None
**Meet and greet photo**: Yes. A Photopass photographer is present.
**Average wait times:** Up to 90 minutes

The Princess Pavilion is home to all your favourite princesses and this is your chance to meet them, chat, play, get an autograph and take some photos. You will only see one princess at the end of the line and there is no way of knowing who this will be in advance. If you want to meet another princess you will need to re-queue.

Important note: During most of the year, there is a normal stand-by line to wait in – you walk in, wait in the queue line and then meet a princess. However, at peak times in order to enter the Pavilion you must first obtain a reservation ticket (located to the left of the pavilion). Be sure to have all your park tickets with you when obtaining this reservation. Return at the time on the reservation and you will be allowed entry into the Pavilion – times vary wildly even with a reservation and the time waiting in the queue can vary from under 10 minutes to up to 90 minutes. When the reservation system is in place, tickets are usually gone by lunchtime. This is a reservation to meet the princesses and not a Fastpass, so it does not affect your other Fastpass selections.

## Le Carrousel de Lancelot:
**Fastpass**: No
**Minimum Height**: None
**On-ride photo**: No
**Ride length:** 2 minutes
**Average wait times:** Under 30 minutes.
**Loading:** 90 guests per ride - About 1500 guests per hour.

This is a beautiful, vintage carrousel that is sure to create memories for everyone of every age. The carrousel is lined with beautiful golden horses, and is a joy to ride for every member of the family. Whether you want to go along with the theme of Lancelot's carrousel or prefer to think of it as the carrousel from Mary Poppins, it is sure to be a fun-filled family adventure.

## Dumbo the Flying Elephant:

**Fastpass**: No
**Minimum Height:** None
**On-ride photo:** No
**Ride length:** Around 1 minute 30 seconds
**Average wait times:** 90 to 120 minutes
**Loading:** 32 guests at a time - 600 to 650 guests per hour.

Step aboard and fly through the skies with Dumbo!

Dumbo is one of the most popular rides in the whole of Disneyland Paris across the two parks. Situated right in the center of Fantasyland it offers amazing views of the surrounding area, as well as being a whole lot of fun. In front of the seats in each flying elephant there is a lever that allows you to lift your Dumbo up or down. You can fly up to 7 meters in the air – that is 23 feet!

Due to the ride's popularity amongst both children and adults alike, its slow loading nature and low capacity, this ride has very long queues all day long. Try to ride it during the parade, Extra Magic Hours, or the beginning or end of the day for the shortest waits. As you can see in the statistics, it handles less than 1000 guests an hour; in comparison 'it's a small world' handles three times as many guests in a single hour.

## The Adventures of Pinocchio:

**Fastpass**: No
**Minimum Height:** None
**On-ride photo**: No
**Ride length:** 2 minutes
**Average wait times:** Between 20 – 45 minutes.
**Loading**: 6 guests per vehicle, 18 vehicles - About 2500 guests an hour.

Ride through a retelling of the story of Pinocchio and see the tales from the book come to life in front of you. There are a few clever effects inside the ride and as with the film, there are also some darker moments that may frighten younger children, though these do pass by quickly and are generally fine for most children.
This ride is not a major attraction like Peter Pan's flight but it still draws in moderately sized queues due to the popularity of the character.

# Casey Jr: The Circus Train:

**Fastpass**: No
**Minimum Height**: None
**On-ride photo:** No
**Ride length:** 2 minutes
**Average wait times:** 20 to 45 minutes
**Loading**: 34 guests per train, 2 trains - About 1400 guests an hour.

Based on the character from Dumbo, Casey Junior is the little circus train that will take you on a ride around many classic Disney films. This is a great ride for the whole family, and although it is not technically a rollercoaster it can be a good way of seeing whether the kids (or adults) are up to a slightly rougher coaster - though this ride is still very tame compared to the likes of Big Thunder Mountain. However, there is no height restriction here meaning that everyone can ride this attraction.

You will whizz by castles and other story pieces retelling you some of Disney's classic tales during your tour. For a more leisurely view of these same scenes try the Storybook Canal Boats ride located next door to this ride.

Note that adults may feel a bit cramped on this ride - and two adults next to each other will have to squeeze in tightly!

Unfortunately the ride is often closed or only opened for limited periods during the off-seasons. When the ride is open, this attraction usually closes two to three hours before the rest of Fantasyland.

**Top Tip**: If you want a specific seat ask the Cast Members and they can accommodate you. You can ride at the front by the engine, in a cage, in an open-air carriage or backwards.

## Le Pays des Contes de Fees / Storybook Canal Boats:

**Fastpass**: No
**Minimum Height**: None
**On-ride photo:** No
**Ride length:** 7 minutes
**Average wait times:** Less than 20 minutes
**Loading**: 16 guests per boat, 20 boats - About 2700 guests an hour.

This is a great relaxing ride on a boat past models of classic childhood tales. Along the journey you will see scenes from the Little Mermaid, Hansel and Grettel, the Wizard of Oz, Aladdin's Cave, and much more. It is a nice, relaxing change from some of the busier attractions in the park and makes for some great photo opportunities. This attraction almost always has low wait times, as many people do not know this section of the park even exists and it has a high hourly capacity.

When the ride is open, this attraction usually closes two to three hours before the rest of Fantasyland.

## Mad Hatter's Teacups
**Fastpass**: No
**Minimum Height**: None
**On-ride photo:** No
**Ride length:** 2 minutes
**Average wait times:** Under 30 minutes
**Loading**: 4 guests per teacup, 18 teacups - About 1000 guests an hour.

Hop inside one of the teacups from Alice in Wonderland and go for a wild spin. The ride functions much like any other teacup ride around the world, where you have a wheel at the centre of the cup and you can turn it to spin yourself round faster, or leave it alone and have a more relaxing spin.

## Meet Mickey Mouse
**Fastpass**: No
**Minimum Height**: None
**Attraction photo:** Yes
**Length:** 1-2 minutes with Mickey
**Average wait times:** 60 - 90 minutes
**Loading**: One group at a time with Mickey.

What if you had the opportunity to meet Mickey himself in a private setting? Well, this is your chance. Mickey is preparing backstage for his next magic show and you have the chance to meet him. The queue line itself is rather boring but there are short films playing on a big screen featuring the main cheese himself to ease the wait.

Once you reach the front of the queue you will be taken to a room with Mickey inside. Here you can meet Mickey, have a chat, get an autograph and take some photos. You are welcome to take your own photos and/or ask the Cast Member present to help you. In addition, there is a Disney photographer there who will also take an official photo, which can be purchased at the exit of the attraction.

## Dining:

**Auberge de Cendrillon** – Table Service restaurant with the Disney Princesses. Adult menu priced at €66 (£55) and children's menu priced at €37 (£31). This meal can be pre-booked and pre-paid as part of a Disneyland Paris package.

**Au Chalet de la Marionette** – Counter Service restaurant. Menus priced at €11 to €14, children's menus priced at €8.50.

**Pizzeria Bella Notte** – Counter Service restaurant. Menus priced at €12-15, children's menus €8.50. Serves pizza, rigatoni pasta and lasagna.

**Toad Hall Restaurant** Counter Service restaurant. Menus priced at €11-15, children's menus €8.50. Serves fish and chips, and chicken sandwiches.

**The Old Mill** – Snack location serving waffles (gaufres) with and without chocolate (€3.80-€4), crisps at €2.30, cake at €4, ice creams at €3.50 to €4, and hot and cold drinks.

**Fantasia Gelati** – Snack location which serves Italian-style scoop ice cream. €2.50 to €4 per ice cream, €3 for a hot drink.

# Discoveryland:

Take a look into the future... from the past. Discoveryland is inspired by retro-futuristic visions of space and beyond. Some of the park's most popular and thrilling attractions are located in this land.

## Attractions:

The major attractions in this land include: **Space Mountain: Mission 2**, **Buzz Lightyear Laser Blast**, **Star Tours** and **Captain EO**. There are also **Orbitron**, **Les Mysteres de Nautilus** (a walkthrough attraction based on 20,000 leagues under the sea), **Autopia**, the **Videopolis Theatre** (Closed until 11$^{th}$ July 2015) and the **Disneyland Railroad Discoveryland Station.**

## Space Mountain: Mission 2 (Closed for Refurbishment until 24$^{th}$ July 2015)

**Fastpass**: Yes
**Minimum Height**: 1.32m
**On-ride photo**: Yes
**Ride length:** 2 minutes 18 seconds
**Average wait times:** 60 to 90 minutes
**Loading**: 2 guests per row, 2000 guests per hour.

Space Mountain: Mission 2 is an incredible rollercoaster through space, and in our opinion the best coaster in the whole of Disneyland Paris. It is the only Space Mountain in the world to have inversions and loops, as well as a high-speed launch.

This is the grandest and roughest of all the Space Mountain rides around the world and the building truly is the centerpiece for the whole of Discoveryland. It is stunning.

The current version of the ride is Space Mountain: Mission 2. For the first twelve years the ride was originally called *De La Terre à la Lune* and in 2005 it closed for a major refurbishment. Although the ride's track layout was kept the same, many of the indoor pieces and effects, as well as the soundtrack, have changed to give the riders a truly immersive experience.

As you soar through space you will come across comets, supernovas, meteorites and more, before landing back in Discoveryland. A must-do attraction!

**Important Note:** Space Mountain is closed from 12$^{th}$ January 2015 to 24$^{th}$ July 2015 for a lengthy refurbishment.

## Star Tours:

**Fastpass**: Yes
**Minimum Height**: 1.02m
**On-ride photo**: No

**Ride length**: About 5 minutes
**Average wait time**: 15 to 45 minutes
**Loading**: 40 riders per StarSpeeder 3000, 6 vehicles. About 2100 people an hour.

Star Wars fans will fall in love with Star Tours, but the attraction is equally accessible and fun to those who have never seen the series of films. This is a definite must-do attraction.

Once you step into the interior portion of the queue line, you will enter an intergalactic spaceport, with adverts for various destinations and overhead announcements of flights leaving. As you travel through the terminal you will see Star-Speeders (your transport vehicle), an alien air traffic control station, R2-D2, C3PO, and many robots hard at work to make your journey to space unforgettable.

Cast Members will split you into groups at the end of the queue line, where you will then board your StarSpeeder vehicle for your space tour to the forest moon of Endor.

Almost the entirety of the dialogue is in French but it is the visuals along with the movement that really matter here; the simulator does feel incredibly realistic and is a great ride.

Be advised that if you are prone to motion sickness or are scared of confined spaces, Star Tours will most probably not be appropriate for you.

**Top Tip:** If you want a milder ride ask to be seated at the front row of the vehicle (which is technically in the middle of the vehicle and thereby reduces the tilting sensations). For a more thrilling experience, ask to be sat in the back row, which really shakes you about, tossing you around in your seat.

**Top Tip 2**: When park attendance is low, Fastpass is not offered at this attraction.

## Buzz Lightyear Laser Blast:

**Fastpass**: Yes
**Minimum Height:** None
**On-ride photo:** Yes
**Ride length**: 5 minutes
**Average wait times:** 60 to 90 minutes
**Loading:** 2 guests per Space Cruiser.

Step aboard the XP-41 Space Cruisers and get ready for some action. Use the onboard laser guns to shoot at the targets around you – you will be helping out Buzz Lightyear and racking up points as you shoot the different targets. Different targets are worth different amounts of points and there are even some hidden targets, which allow you to score thousands of bonus points in one go.

In addition to shooting, you can also change the direction of the Space Cruiser you are in by spinning it around with a joystick in the middle.

At the end of the ride, the person with the most points wins. It is competitive, fun and endlessly re-rideable – it is also a great family adventure with no minimum height limit. If you buy an attraction photo at the end, you can get the scores printed on the photos as a souvenir too!

**Top Tip**: The highest scoring target is placed when you are directly in front of Zurg – shoot his medallion to get an insane amount of points and easily max out the high score.

## Autopia:

**Fastpass**: No
**Minimum Height**: Riders under 0.81m may not ride. Riders between 0.81m and 1.32m must be accompanied by someone over the 1.32m height minimum. Riders over 1.32m may ride alone.
**On-ride photo**: No
**Ride length**: About 5 minutes
**Average wait times:** 60 to 90 minutes
**Loading**: 2 Guests per car, up to 60 cars - Between 750 and 1500 guests per hour depending on number of guests per car and number of lanes open.

Hop aboard one of these little cars and take it for a spin around Discoveryland. This attraction is hugely popular with kids, particularly with little boys who get to drive a car for the very first time. The cars are guided on rails so guests can not really go too far wrong but the little ones (and bigger ones too) can steer and accelerate around the track and race others. The ride is open to people of all ages and is definitely worth a visit - good family fun.

**Fun fact:** The cars in Autopia travel up to 2000km per day!

# Orbitron - Machines Volantes:

**Fastpass**: No
**Minimum Height**: None
**On-ride photo**: No
**Ride length**: 1 minute 30 seconds
**Average wait times:** 30 to 60 minutes
**Loading**: 2 Guests per spaceship, 12 spaceships - About 360 guests per hour.

Soar above Discoveryland in your very own spaceship. This is a spinning-type ride similar to Dumbo in Fantasyland. However, the ships here can go much higher and tilt both inwards and outwards and at the top you can really feel some speed. It is a lot of fun but we would not say it is a must-do attraction because of its similarity to other attractions such as Dumbo and Flying Carpets Over Agrabah.
**Note**: Despite ride operators wanting to maximise capacity, two adults can fit in one spaceship but it will *not* be comfortable – we recommend asking for one spaceship per person if you are two adults; an adult and a child should easily fit in the spaceships.

## Captain EO:

**Fastpass**: No
**Minimum Height**: None
**Show length**: 17 minutes + 7 minute 'making-of' pre-show
**Average wait times**: 30 minutes
**Loading**: 600 Guests per show - shows start about every 20 minutes

For the Michael Jackson fans this is one show not to be missed! Captain EO is a 3D spectacular featuring in-theatre special effects to truly immerse guests. The attraction was one of the originals from when the park opened but it was then replaced by *Honey I Shrunk the Audience* for several years. Captain EO then returned in June 2010 as a tribute following Michael Jackson's death.

*Captain EO* stars Michael Jackson himself, two original songs, a cute storyline, cool costumes and sets and an astounding cast. During the film the characters transform themselves into part of Jackson's band to fight the forces of evil with music! Admittedly the storyline is a little limp and the effects are a little bit old-fashioned but it is still a fun bit of nostalgia.

However, do be prepared for the annoying 'Making of Captain EO' video before being let into the main theatre. This attraction is subject to limited opening hours and dates during non-peak times of the year.

**Fun fact:** *Captain EO* is 17 minutes in length and cost over $30million to make, making it the most expensive film per minute at the time is was created.

## Les Mysteres de Nautilus

Fans of '20,000 Leagues Under the Sea' are sure to love this underwater exploration of the Nautilus. This is a highly detailed themed environment which is a walkthrough area – unless you are a major fan, however, you are unlikely to think very much of this attraction.

### Dining:
There are only two places to eat in Discoveryland:
**Buzz Lightyear's Pizza Planet** - Buffet restaurant. Priced at €20 for adults including unlimited soft drinks and €12 for children including unlimited soft drinks. Note that Pizza Planet is usually only open during peak seasons and weekends.
**Cafe Hyperion (Closed until 11th July 2015)** - Counter service restaurant. Adult menus priced at €11 to €14, and children's menus priced at €8.

## Fireworks in Disneyland Park – Disney Dreams:

Disney theme parks around the world have been renowned for years for ending visitors' days with a bang by lighting up the sky with incredible firework displays. Up until 2012, Disneyland Paris was very much lacking in this department with fireworks only being offered seasonally and with a less than impressive show.

April 2012 saw the arrival of Disneyland Paris' 20$^{th}$ anniversary celebrations and all that changed with the introduction of *Disney Dreams* – a dazzling nighttime spectacular which coordinates music, projections, lasers, water fountains and fireworks.

In addition to Disney Dreams, there are standard fireworks offered at the park offered on select nights throughout the year such as Bastille Day and New Year's Day.

Currently Disney Dreams is performed every night at park closing at Disneyland Park for the foreseeable future. The show runs for 22-minutes. After the fireworks Main Street USA will remain open until about an hour after the park closes.

During the Christmas season the show changes completely to *Disney Dreams of Christmas* which celebrates the most wonderful time of the year. A Halloween version of Disney Dreams is also in the works and may debut in 2015 but there is no confirmation of this.

Walt Disney Studios Park does not offer a nighttime show throughout the year, except on New Year's Eve. Lake Disney located by the hotels also offers fireworks during select dates around Bonfire Night and on New Year's Eve too – you do not require park admission for these events at Lake Disney.

# Disney Dreams Viewing Guide:

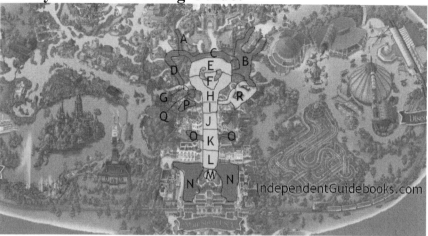

Disney Dreams is primarily a projections show that relies heavily on you having a view of the front of Sleeping Beauty Castle. Although the fireworks can be seen from across the park, you will not get a concept of the storyline if you are not viewing the front of the castle and the projections on it. This area is also where the lasers can be seen, the fountains and the fire effects, as well as the Second Star to the Right.

You will want to position yourself at the central plaza (hub) area of the park or along Main Street USA for the best view. This is, however, a large area and to help you decide on the best view of Disney Dreams we have created this helpful diagram – note that the zones or areas in the diagram have been created by us and there are no delineations between the areas when you are in the park itself. Below is a detailed analysis of each area:

**Zone A** – Guests are not permitted in this zone during Disney Dreams and its preparations

**Zone B** – Guests are not permitted in the majority of this zone during Disney Dreams. The areas they are permitted in provide a very poor and obstructed view.

**Zone C** – This zone is too close to Sleeping Beauty Castle for your enjoyment. You will miss some or all of the fireworks behind the castle, the projections will also not have their full effect as you will be too close, you will also likely get very wet from the water fountains.

**Zone D** – Views from this area are obstructed by trees, and provide a very off-centre angle with poor visibility.

**Zone E** – This is where guests who arrive early will position themselves. This area provides a decent view of the spectacle and you will be able to see all fireworks and effects. It is however, still too close to the action for you to appreciate the show fully.

**Zone F** – This zone faces Sleeping Beauty Castle head-on and is far back enough to start to provide a good view of the whole show. It is not the perfect view but is very, very good.

**Zone G** – This zone is located off-center, behind and to the left of the Disney dreams control booth. If you position yourself by the railing here you will get a fantastic view of the show – this location can only accommodate a few people.

**Zone H** – This zone provides our favourite views of the show. It is the perfect distance from Sleeping Beauty Castle and if you position yourself by one of the railings that surround the flowerbeds you will have a new perfect view of the show.

**Zone I** – This is another one of our favourite views of the show, which provides a great distance from the castle to see the full show effects whilst not feeling too distant. This area is also usually less crowded than Zone H.

**Zone J, K and L** – These zones are located along Main Street USA and provide an average view of the show. The closer you are to the Castle the better. One positive thing about these zones is that they are usually much less crowded than zones closer to the castle. Be aware that you will see a lot of people in front of you including children on parents' shoulders.

**Zone M** – This zone has to be staked out very early and involves you standing on the bandstand in Town Square – there is very, very limited space here but it provides an elevated view over other guests on Main street USA. Specific projections are hard to see from this distance but the unique view of the show from this location makes it worth considering and one of our favourite gems. And at the end of the show – you are right near the exit to the park and ahead of the crowds.

**Zones N and O** – These zones offer no visibility of the show at all and are strongly discouraged.

**Zone P and Q**– This offers views of the show which are obstructed by trees and the Disney Dreams control booth. We do not recommend this location.

**Zone R** – This is a very off centre view and with many trees in front meaning less than OK visibility – this is improved in the winter when there is less foliage but this is still not a great viewing location.

We recommend you find a spot where there is a railing in front of you if possible – this will prevent someone from turning up just as the show starts and obscuring your view. This is especially prevalent among European guests who like to put their children on their shoulders as the show begins, ruining the view for everyone behind them. Equally frustrating can be someone in front of you who decides to film the whole show on his or her phone or camera. Be generally aware of people who appear at the last minute and obstruct your view.

**Top Tip:** In order to get the best spot for Disney Dreams we recommend you show up a minimum of 45 minutes before the show begins. For the Town Square bandstand/gazebo you will usually need to be in place well over an hour in advance.

You can also become part of Disney Dreams with glow-in-the-dark hats, which Disney has dubbed LightEars. They are Mickey ear shaped hats, with LEDs inside them, which change colour and flash in time with the show, so when the castle is coloured blue the hat on your head will turn blue as well. They can be purchased throughout most shopping locations on Main Street U.S.A for €20 each. The effect unfortunately is rather disappointing with about a dozen guests using the hats each night completely negating any impressive effect.

**Top Tip**: One common question that guests ask after the show is "Where are the toilets?" After the show, all lands except Main Street USA will be closed. There are therefore two main toilet locations for you to use – the first, and the least crowded, is located by the Baby Care Centre and Victoria's Home Style Restaurant at the hub of the park (Zone R on the map). The second and infinitely busier location is at the end of Main Street USA and to the right of the Disneyland Railroad station at the Arboretum (Zone N).

## Parades:

*Disney Magic on Parade* is the best way to see all your favourite Disney characters in one place as they parade through Fantasyland, around the castle hub and down Main Street USA.

The parade is performed once per day and the time varies seasonally but is usually at 5:30pm in the peak summer season and 5:00pm for the rest of the year. Characters present in the parade can vary from day to day but you can usually expect to see about fifty different characters and floats, including: the three fairies, Merlin the magician, the fairy godmother, Cinderella and her prince, Snow White and her prince, Anna and Elsa (from Disney's Frozen), Rapunzel and Flynn Rider (from Disney's Tangled), Pinocchio and Gepetto, Alice in Wonderland, The Mad Hatter, The Queen of Hearts, The Green Toy Soldiers, Woody, Buzz, Jessie, Tigger, Eeyore, Piglet, Timon, Pumba, Simba, Baloo and King Louie, Peter Pan and Captain Hook, Mary Poppins and Bert, Mickey, Minnie, Goofy, Chip and Dale, Donald, Duffy the Disney Bear and Tinker Bell.

The most popular place to watch the parade from is from Main Street USA – you will need to secure your spot at least 1 hour before the parade begins if you plan on standing at the front to get the best shots.

The parade will be performed regardless of the weather situation; this means it will take place during light or moderate rain. During heavy rain or the risk of lightning there is the potential for the parade to be cancelled or delayed. In either case, an announcement will be made at the parade start time. Disneyland Paris prefers to delay a parade than to cancel it altogether as it is an important daily event in the park.

Visitors to other Disney theme parks worldwide may be familiar with the concept of a nighttime parade. Although, Disneyland Paris did for many years host a nighttime parade this form of entertainment is no longer offered.

In addition during seasonal events such as Spring, Halloween and Christmas, there are smaller two to three float parades (dubbed cavalcades) performed several times a day.

Chapter 8
# Walt Disney Studios Park

Walt Disney Studios Park is the second, and newest, park at Disneyland Paris. Here you can go behind the scenes and experience the magic of the movies. The theme park opened in 2002 and has expanded greatly over the years. In general, the park targets adolescents and adults more than young children and contains several thrilling attractions. There are also several attractions for the younger family members too.

Despite its expansion over the years, you would still be hard-pressed to spend an entire day in this park due to the limited number of attractions. Disneyland Paris has stated that expanding the park and improving its offerings is very important to them. In 2014 *Ratatouille: The Adventure* was unveiled, a unique 3D trackless dark ride, but many more attractions are to come in the next few years. At 4.5 million visitors per year, the park is Europe's third most popular but still only receives less than half the number of visitors that its big brother, Disneyland Park, gets next door.

The park is divided into five main areas: Front Lot, Toon Studio, Production Courtyard, Toy Story Playland and Backlot.

# Front Lot:

This is the entrance area to Walt Disney Studios and home to **Disney Studio 1** - a building recreated to be like Tinsel Town which every guest must walk through to get to the rest of the park - inside it are several shops and restaurants. Disney Studio 1 is the equivalent of Main Street in Disneyland Park. Sometimes there is street entertainment that happens here. This area often offers face painting too (priced at €10 to €14). It is also home to Studio Services (guest services) where you can get assistance.

**Dining**:
You will find **Restaurant en Coulisse** (Counter service, menus €11-€14, children €8) running on the right-hand side of Studio 1 behind several facades of famous movie sets. There is also a small stand called **The Hep Cat Corner** (Snacks, hot and cold drinks - €3 to €4, donut and drink - €5.50, ice creams - €3 to €4)

# Production Courtyard:

**Attractions:**
Some of the parks biggest attractions are located in Production Courtyard: **The Twilight Zone: Tower of Terror, Cinemagique, Studio Tram Tour: Behind the Magic, Stitch Live!** and **Disney Junior Live**.

# The Twilight Zone: Tower of Terror

**Fastpass**: Yes
**Minimum Height**: 1.02m
**On-ride photo**: Yes
**Ride length**: 2 minutes 25 seconds + Pre-show (Total experience = about 15 minutes)
**Average wait times**: 60 to 90 minutes

The Twilight Zone: Tower of Terror transports you to the fifth dimension as you enter an elevator for the ride of your life. During the ride you will see some incredible special effects and experience what it is like to drop 183 feet straight down again and again.

Disney summarises the ride nicely: "You are the passengers on a most uncommon elevator about to ascend into your very own episode of...The Twilight Zone. One stormy night long ago, five people stepped through the door of an elevator and into a nightmare. That door is opening once again, and this time it's opening for you."

You board a service elevator; learn about the ghostly past of the hotel and then you 'drop in' for yourself. The elevator is pulled down faster than gravity causing you to come out of your seat – good job there are seatbelts. The motors on this ride are very powerful and within a split second the elevator changes from going up to down creating a sensation unlike any other ride.

The atmosphere inside is truly immersive and is possibly the best theming in the whole of Disneyland Paris. The pre-show is great and you will really feel the tension before you plummet. In addition, the Cast Members who work on this ride really add to the atmosphere through their creepy acting.

This is a fun ride, but it is an intense experience that WILL have you screaming.

Fastpass is recommended as the queue can be long but be aware that by using Fastpass you will miss out on a lot of the detail in the interior queue line. We also recommend that first time riders buy the on-ride photo for their reactions. It will be worth it.

## Stitch Live!:

**Fastpass**: No
**Minimum Height:** None
**Show length:** 15 minutes
**Average wait times**: Shows at set times
**Loading:** 200 guests per show

It is time for us earthlings to communicate with Stitch in his space ship in this fun show. As a guest you enter a special transmission room where adults sit on benches and the kids sit out the front. Before you know it a Cast Member with special space access will connect to Stitch and you will be speaking with him live. Stitch is curious about how the earth works, so he will ask all sorts of questions to learn about our planet. All in all, this attraction is great fun, although Stitch can be a bit mean to some of the adults.

## Disney Junior Live on Stage!:

**Fastpass**: No
**Minimum Height:** None
**Show length:** 25 minutes
**Average wait times**: Shows at set times
**Loading:** 450 guests per show – most spots are on the floor with some limited bench seating.

This show is definitely targeted towards the smaller kids in your party. Join Mickey, Donald and the Gang (represented in puppet form) as they prepare for Minnie's birthday party – and just like in the TV show, they need your help to succeed. This toddler-friendly show will have your kids clapping, running around and dancing and is sure to be a highlight for fans of the Disney Junior show. Separate English and French shows are performed throughout the day and guests can see the next show time outside the attraction as well as how many seats remain.

**Top Tip**: Jake (from the Neverland Pirates) & Sofia The First can both be seen and met in the pre-show area of this attraction.
**Top Tip 2**: The whole building is air-conditioned which makes it a good place to cool down during the warmer months. Equally, because it is indoors it is a good place to escape the rain and cold.

## Studio Tram Tour: Behind the Magic:

**Fastpass**: No
**Minimum Height:** None
**On-ride photo**: No
**Ride length:** 15 minutes
**Average wait times**: 30 to 60 minutes
**Loading:** 168 guests per tram, up to 4 trams – Up to 2000 guests an hour.

Hop aboard the Studio Tram Tour and see authentic props and vehicles from well-known movies, and see sets close-up. During the ride you will experience fire, water and earthquakes close up and see scenes from movies unfold in front of your very eyes – plus you will be part of the action too! Commentary is provided in English and French via screens on the tram. This is a great family adventure that everyone can experience. It features a unique Reign of Fire scene not found in the Walt Disney World version, as well as the impressive Catastrophe Canyon.

## Cinemagique:

**Fastpass**: No
**Show length**: 25 minutes
**Average wait times**: Only at scheduled times - arrive early.
**Loading:** 1100 Guests per show.

For all the lovers of movies, Disneyland Paris has a little trick up its sleeve for you - Cinemagique! Take a trip through time and see some clips from classic movies, as well as some newer additions mixed together in a hugely entertaining manner. Expect more than you bargained for with this show featuring live actors as well as on-screen characters, combined to make a truly unforgettable experience you will want to watch again and again. This is a truly 4D spectacular mixing the world around you and on-screen entertainment. Make it a point to stop by and watch this show. Arrive at least 15 minutes before the show starts in order to get a good seat. The centre of the theatre offers the best view.

**Top Tip**: Spoiler - Sitting too close to the front may startle young children, as there is a loud explosion towards the start of the show.

**Dining:**
**Restaurant des Stars** - Buffet restaurant. Adult buffet – €25.50 with no drinks included or €29 with one drink; children's buffet priced at €16 with one soft drink included.
**Hollywood and Lime** – Snack location. Drinks - €3 to €4, desserts - €3 to €4, teatime treats also available.

# Backlot:

## Attractions:
The Backlot of the park is where you will find **Rock n' Rollercoaster**, **Moteurs...Action! Stunt Show** and **Armageddon: Special Effects/Les Effets Speciaux**.

## Rock 'n' Rollercoaster: Starring Aerosmith:

**Fastpass**: Yes
**Minimum Height**: 1.20m
**On-ride photo**: Yes
**Ride length**: 1 minutes 20 seconds
**Average wait times**: Under 60 minutes
**Loading**: 2 guests per row, 24 guests per train – 1800 guests per hour.

Hop aboard the SoundTrackers and take a high-speed ride through an Aerosmith music video at over 55mph in this rollercoaster experience. The ride will take you through three inversions, a catapult launch to maximum speed in under 2.5 seconds, and 5Gs of G-Force.

In the pre-show you will see lifelike holograms of Aerosmith getting you ready to shoot a music video. Then it is time to go through to the loading area where you will see the trains being launched to just under 100kmph in just a couple of seconds. For each launch there is a short light show, fog and a countdown. This launch looks much more intimidating than it actually feels on the ride.

After the launch, you will notice that each SoundTracker is equipped with speakers all around your body including around your head for ultimate musical enjoyment. There are several inversions, but we applaud the ride for how smooth and comfortable it is.

Each SoundTracker has songs preloaded onto it and each plays different Aerosmith songs from the Rock n Rollercoaster song list. The lights and effects on the ride change colour and sequence depending on your vehicle. Feel free to sing along to "Young lust", "Dude looks like a lady", "Walk this way" as well as countless others.

This ride almost always has surprisingly low wait times, even when the rest of the park is relatively packed. Coaster fans: do it!

**Top Tip 1:** It is good to know that when park attendance is low Fastpass is not offered for this attraction.

**Top Tip 2**: Wait times will peak significantly throughout the day as the "Moteurs… Action" stunt show, located right next door, finishes and dumps 3000 guests at a time into the park. Many of these guests will go directly to Rock n' Rollercoaster. If you see the show guests exiting we recommend you come back later as the wait time posted will not yet be accurate and the waits will be unnecessarily long.

# Moteurs, Action! Stunt Show Spectacular:

**Fastpass**: No
**Show length**: 40 minutes
**Average wait times**: At scheduled times - arrive early for the best seats.
**Loading**: 3000 Guests per show (up to 3 shows per day)

At *Moteurs, Action!* sit back and watch movie stunts be performed in front of your very eyes – and then learn how they are done!

This attraction is a major draw for many of Disneyland Paris' visitors and pulls in thousands of guests at a time meaning that queues for other attractions will be lighter when shows are on. Arrive around 30 minutes before the show to get a good seat - the middle seating section provides the best view and the lower down you are, the closer you are to the action. Although all seats do have a good view, being closer to the action really can make the experience more enjoyable.

Unfortunately, due to several incidents, the show has been toned down several times since its opening and several of the big stunts have been removed which means that much of the excitement is now gone. We expect the show to be completely overhauled or removed over the coming years.

## Armageddon: Les Effets Speciaux:
**Fastpass**: No
**Minimum Height:** None
**On-ride photo**: No
**Show length**: 20 minutes (15 minutes pre-show, 5 minute show experience)
**Average wait times**: Less than 30 minutes
**Loading**: 200 Guests per show (up to 3 shows per day)

Armageddon is really what the Walt Disney Studios Park is about - getting you to experience what it is like to be in a film. At this attraction, you are on the set of 'Armageddon' on the Russian Space Station. Your job is to be an extra - to act and scream as directed as you are plunged into space.

During the pre-show, the director will ask you to practice acting scared as you watch various scenes from the film. Then it is time for the filming itself, as you are taken to the Space Station set. Once on the "hot set", right on cue a meteor shower hits the space station and it is all fun and games from there onwards.

**Spoilers**: Once the meteor shower starts guests should be ready for collapsing ceilings, very loud noises, sparks, fire, water, a dropping floor and much more. If you have young kids with you, we recommend you do not position them around the centre of the set as a huge fireball is launched twice here.

## Dining:
**Cafe des Cascadeurs** – Quick service location. Salad - €8, adult menus priced at €13 to €15, children's menus - €9, drinks. Desserts and ice creams are also served.
**Blockbuster Cafe** – Quick service location. A la carte sandwiches priced at €7, pizzas at €9, salads and pasta at €7 to €8, drinks and desserts are also served priced at between €3 and €4.

# Toon Studio:

## Attractions:
Discover the magic behind Disney cartoons and animation in this area of the park, from Disney classics to Pixar favourites. Attractions in this area of the park include: **Art of Disney Animation, Animagique, Flying Carpets over Agrabah, Crush's Coaster, Cars Quatre Roues Rallye** and **Ratatouille: The Adventure**.

## Art of Disney Animation:
**Fastpass**: No
**Show length**: 20 minutes + optional drawing time
**Average wait times**: Less than 30 minutes
**Loading**: 225 Guests per tour - 1800 guests an hour.

If you fancy seeing more behind the scenes magic and learning about how the Disney films are animated, this is the place to visit.

The first pre-show room of this attraction shows how animation has evolved with models, videos, and replicas of animation equipment. Here can see one of only two multi-plane cameras in the world. These were used to create some of the original Disney classics and they are true masterpieces. Also in this room, a large screen plays a video featuring Roy O Disney. You are then ushered into a cinema.

In the cinema you will see clips showing how animated films can arouse emotions within their audience. Finally, you are taken to another room where there are theatre-style seats and a live animator who will guide you through how characters are created from scratch to the final product – Mushu, the dragon, is also on hand to help.

After this demonstration you ushered into a final room which contains several props and paintings. This room allows you to exit back into park – alternatively you can stick around for one of the drawing classes where an animator will teach you how to draw one of the Disney characters. These drawing classes are only available seasonally and at specific times but are a huge amount of fun to take part in.

## Crush's Coaster:

**Fastpass**: No
**Minimum Height**: 1.07m
**On-ride photo**: No
**Ride length**: 2 minutes 20 seconds
**Average wait times**: 90 to 120 minutes
**Loading**: 4 guests per shell, 12 turtle shells - About 900 guests per hour.

Crush wants you to come aboard and journey through the East Australian Current in this fast and thrilling coaster.

Crush's Coaster is a unique attraction and the only of its kind in any Disney theme park worldwide. Guests board turtle shells in groups of four - facing outwards back to back in pairs and prepare to experience a ride you will not forget. Most of the ride is in darkness with bubbles, projections, set pieces and more scattered around the track to give you the feeling of riding the waves with Crush.

Although the ride may seem to marketed at younger kids, do not be fooled - this is a wild, fast ride so read the warning signs outside first. For the thrill seekers among you, some people rate this attraction as the most "thrilling" ride in the whole of Disneyland Paris, so it is a definite must-do!

The ride does not offer Disney's Fastpass service. The lack of Fastpass, accompanied with the popularity of the Finding Nemo characters and the ride's low hourly capacity means that this ride regularly has the longest queue in the entire park (although since Summer 2014, Ratatouille has eased queues at Crush slightly). If you must ride Crush's Coaster do it the first thing in the morning or just before park closing - even on less busy days queues exceed 40 minutes and it is common to see the wait time at over 90 minutes. We recommend that you line up for this attraction as soon as the parks pre-open at 9:30am – it is really the only way to do it without waiting for an extended period of time.

A single rider line is available at this attraction.

**New**: Guests waiting in line for Crush's Coaster can now help the time pass by playing an interactive game on their smartphone. The game is available exclusively in the queue line by connecting to a dedicated Wi-Fi network and opening up your Internet browser. This Wi-Fi connection will only allow access to the game, and will not allow you to browse the Internet. The game is compatible with all touchscreen smartphones and is completely free to play.

## Animagique:
**Fastpass**: No
**Show length**: 20 minutes
**Average wait times**: This show runs at scheduled times.
**Loading**: 1100 guests per performance.

In our opinion, Animagique is the king of all stage shows at Disneyland Paris. Set in an indoor theatre and using black light effects and incredible puppetry, Disney brings its classic films to life in a musical spectacular. See scenes from The Jungle Book, Dumbo, The Lion King and The Little Mermaid, as well as Mickey and Donald themselves. This show is a definite must-see for all ages which is sure to have you singing along and is great for some quality family time. As an added bonus, due to being indoors it is a great shelter from the unpredictable Parisian weather – sun, rain or snow!

**Note**: For the safety of performers, no photography or filming is allowed inside this attraction. This is strictly enforced by Cast Members.

## Flying Carpets over Agrabah:

**Fastpass**: Yes
**Minimum Height**: None
**On-ride photo**: No
**Ride length**: 1 minute 30 seconds
**Average wait times**: Under 20 minutes
**Loading**: 4 guests per flying carpet, 12 flying carpets - About 900 guests per hour.

Board one of Aladdin's flying carpets and get ready to fly over Agrabah. As you soar the skies you will hear the Genie through his director's megaphone telling you how to act on this film set. The ride itself is a simple spinner ride, and is very similar to both Dumbo and Orbitron (at Disneyland Park) – this ride, however, often has much shorter queues. Here you can lower your carpet up and down, as well as tilt it backwards and forwards – have fun!

**Top Tip**: Fastpass is not offered at this attraction when park attendance is low.

# Cars Quatre Roues Rallye:

**Fastpass**: No
**Minimum Height**: None
**On-ride photo**: No
**Ride length**: 1 minute 30 seconds
**Average wait times**: 30 to 60 minutes
**Loading**: 4 guests car, 12 cars - About 900 guests per hour.

Hop on for the spin of lifetime on Route 66 with characters from Disney Pixar's 'Cars'.

*Cars* fans will enjoy the queue line which is filled with details immersing you into the world of Radiator Springs. There are even life-size models of Lightning McQueen and Mater for you to take photos of.

The ride itself, functions using a very similar ride system as the teacups ride in Disneyland Park but you spin a little faster in this version, and it always looks like your going to collide with the other cars which adds to the fun - and terror. Ride vehicles cannot accommodate 4 adults each, but rather either 2 adults and 2 children, or 3 adults.

# Ratatouille: The Adventure:

**Fastpass**: Yes
**Minimum Height**: None
**On-ride photo**: No
**Ride length**: Approximately 5 minutes
**Average wait times**: 90 to 180 minutes
**Loading**: Vehicles for six people, two rows of 3. About 1800 guests per hour.

Launched in Summer 2014, *Ratatouille: The Adventure* is a new thrilling experience at Disneyland Paris that is designed to be experienced by the whole family. Here you board a 'ratmobile' and travel through Paris' streets, rooftops and kitchens in a 4D immersive ride featuring giant video screens, scents, water effects and much more. This is the first ride in Europe to not use a fixed track and instead the vehicles all take different paths meaning that you can have a slightly different experience each time you ride. A Single Rider Line is available for this attraction.

## Dining:

**Bistrot Chez Remy** – Table service restaurant. Set menus only – €29.90 for starter and a main course, €39.90 for a starter, main course, dessert and a drink, €45.99 for a starter and a main course from a wider selection, or €59,99 for the Menu Gusteau which includes a starter, main course, dessert and a drink with premium choices. A Premium Meal Plan voucher can be exchanged for The Gusteau menu option.

# Toy Story Playland:

## Attractions:

Toy Story Playland is technically a 'land within a land' that shrinks you down to the size of a toy. This area is part of Toon Studio. There are three attractions in this area: **Toy Soldiers Parachute Drop**, **RC Racer** and **Slinky Dog Zigzag Spin**.

## Toy Soldiers Parachute Drop:

**Fastpass**: No
**Minimum Height**: 0.81m
**On-ride photo**: No
**Ride length**: 1 minute
**Average wait times**: 60 to 90 minutes
**Loading**: 6 guests per parachute, 6 parachutes - About 720 guests per hour.

Board one of the Toy Soldiers' parachute and get ready to soar up into the sky and then sail back to the ground again and again. This is a great family ride and has become a new rite of passage for many.

This can also be a good way of gauging whether you like the sensation of dropping and therefore whether *The Twilight Zone: Tower of Terror* is something you will want to experience or not, but this ride is *much* tamer.

A single rider queue is available for guests wishing to board individually.

## RC Racer:

**Fastpass**: No
**Minimum Height**: 1.20m
**On-ride photo**: No
**Ride length**: 1 minute
**Average wait times**: 60 to 90 minutes
**Loading**: 20 guests per ride (5 rows of 4 people) - About 600 guests per hour.

Hop on the RC car from Pixar's Toy Story and feel the wind in your hair. The ride looks significantly more intimidating than it actually is and the sensation is not anywhere near as scary as it looks. In fact, this ride is great fun and a good adrenaline rush – it is often likened to being a tamer version of the swinging pirate ships found at many theme parks.

A single rider queue is available for guests wishing to save time and board individually.

## Slinky Dog Zigzag Spin:

**Fastpass**: No
**Minimum Height**: None
**On-ride photo**: No
**Ride length**: 1 minutes 30 seconds
**Average wait times**: 30 to 60 minutes
**Loading**: 40 guests per ride - About 800 guests per hour.

Hop on Slinky Dog and enjoy yourself as you spin round and round in circles getting increasingly faster and faster. This is a fun family-friendly attraction.

## Fireworks and Parades:

Live entertainment at Walt Disney Studios Park is limited to the stage shows on offer such as *Cinemagique*, *Animagique* and *Moteurs, Action*. Unfortunately this park does not have a daytime or nighttime parade, nor does it have a nighttime show or fireworks. You will find *Disney Dreams,* the nightly fireworks show, at Disneyland Park.

Chapter 9
# Fastpass

One service that often grabs people's attention when visiting Disneyland Paris is Fastpass. Many theme parks have a service which allows guests to skip the long lines but Disneyland Paris offers their Fastpass system for free.

By using a Fastpass you will be able to board selected rides with little to no wait by reserving a slot in advance for a particular ride. Until it is time for your ride slot, you can do something else such as shop, dine, watch a show or experience another attraction.

## How to use Fastpass at Disneyland Paris:

1. Find a ride that offers Fastpass, you can identify these by the little "FP" logo on the park maps. It is helpful to know which attractions offer Fastpasses in advance by reading through this guide book and looking at park maps.
2. Go to a Fastpass-enabled attraction. There will be two entrances to the ride – the standard "stand-by" entrance where you can simply queue up and ride, and Fastpass ticket entrance (e.g. 45 minutes). Nearby there will be the Fastpass distribution area with large Fastpass machines and clocks which show you the current return slot for Fastpass reservations (e.g. 14:15 to 14:45).
3. If the standard queue time is short, go straight onto the ride by using the standby entrance. If the queue is longer than you are prepared to wait, then this is your chance to use the Fastpass system by making a reservation. In general if the waiting time is less than 30 minutes we recommend you wait in the standard line and not use the Fastpass. This is because Fastpasses often require you to backtrack across the park negating any time savings.
4. The Fastpass return time clocks will display a 30-minute time window - e.g. 14:15 - 14:45. This time will be printed on any Fastpasses obtained now. You must return between the two times to use the Fastpass ticket.

5. Go to the Fastpass machines located near the entrance of the attraction and swipe your park ticket or your annual pass on the reader. For e-tickets and tickets with a barcode on the back, scan these using the barcode reader.
6. Once you have scanned your ticket put your park ticket away safely. The machine will print a paper Fastpass telling you what time to return: this is the same time window that was shown on the board above the entrance. Keep this Fastpass safe.
7. Feel free to do whatever you want until that time - e.g. Have a meal, wander around the park or experience another ride or show.
8. Return to the ride during the time window shown on your Fastpass, with your Fastpass in hand and enter through the Fastpass entrance. This will be clearly signposted but if you are unsure, simply ask a Cast Member.
9. Hand your Fastpass to the Cast Member at the Fastpass entrance who will keep it. Now, you can experience the ride within a few minutes skipping the entire regular queue – the wait time with a Fastpass is often under 5 minutes but can be up to 15 minutes.

## List of FASTPASS attractions:
## Disneyland Park:
- Space Mountain: Mission 2
- Buzz Lightyear Laser Blast
- Star Tours
- Peter Pan's Flight
- Indiana Jones et le Temple du Peril
- Big Thunder Mountain

## Walt Disney Studios Park:
- The Twilight Zone: Tower of Terror
- Rock 'N' Rollercoaster: Starring Aerosmith
- Flying Carpets over Agrabah
- Ratatouille: The Adventure

## Extra tips:
1. Some rides only offer Fastpasses when there are a certain amount of guests at the park whereas others offer Fastpasses every day. The rides that may not have Fastpasses during your visit if you visit outside of peak times include: Star Tours, Indiana Jones et le Temple du Peril, Rock 'N' Rollercoaster: Starring Aerosmith and Flying Carpets over Agrabah (only at peak times). Some, none, or all of these rides may have Fastpasses depending on attendance. The reason Fastpass will be disabled on these rides is because it would provide no time savings if it were activated.
2. There are a limited number of Fastpass tickets for each ride every day. Fastpass tickets move in 5 minute slots so after all the Fastpasses for 11:00-11:30 are distributed, the next return time will be 11:05-11:35. Due to the limited amount of Fastpasses, these tickets do run out on popular rides. This is especially likely to happen on *Peter Pan's Flight*, *Big Thunder Mountain*, *Buzz Lightyear Laser Blast* and *Ratatouille: The Adventure*. Some of these rides will have distributed all Fastpasses for the entire day by lunchtime.
3. Every Disneyland Paris entry ticket and annual pass includes access to the Fastpass service – it is a system open to every guest. You do not have to pay for these under any circumstances, nor do you have to stay at a certain hotel or have a certain ticket.
4. You can usually only hold one Fastpass at a time. Once you have used one, you can obtain your next one. However, there are a few exceptions. See the points below on how to hold two Fastpasses at a time.
5. As soon as your Fastpass return time window opens and it is time to ride, you can pick up another Fastpass for a different attraction even if you have not physically used your current Fastpass yet. For example if you have a Fastpass to be used on *Space Mountain* between 2:00pm-2:30pm and it is 2:05om, you can pick up a Fastpass for another ride such as *Star Tours* (nearby) from 2:00pm and then ride *Space Mountain*. This way, you are riding Space Mountain whilst

virtually queuing for Star Tours, saving you even more time!
6. Cast Members will usually allow you to use your Fastpass after the time it says it is valid for - though definitely not before. This is at a Cast Member's discretion so do not count on it for sure. Though we have never been refused entry, it could happen!
7. *Tower of Terror* and *Rock N Rollercoaster* both feature a pre-show video that you must sit through. This can add up to 15 minutes of queuing time, so if anyone is waiting for you, please alert them to this. *Buzz Lightyear* and *Space Mountain* will also often be a 15-minute wait before boarding. The Fastpass line for *Ratatouille: The Adventure* can also easily reach 15 minutes. On other attractions you should be riding in less than 5 minutes with a Fastpass.
8. The Fastpass system is not connected between different parks. Therefore, it is possible to hold a Fastpass for a Walt Disney Studios Park attraction and a Fastpass for a Disneyland Park attraction at the same time, and use them as their times become available. Be aware that from one end of Disneyland Park to the other end of Walt Disney Studios Park will take you between 20 to 30 minutes to walk. You must hold a 2-park "hopper" ticket to enter both parks and take advantage of the Fastpass service at both parks – be sure to ask for your hand to be stamped at the exit of the park so you can transfer back and forth between parks.
9. If your return time is more than two hours away, then you are allowed to obtain another Fastpass two hours after you picked up the first. E.g. You pick up a Fastpass at 10:00am for Space Mountain and the return time is 3:00pm-3:30pm, as 3:00pm is longer than 2 hours away from when you got your Fastpass, you will be able to get a Fastpass at midday (two hours after 10:00am). Remember, if in doubt, you can always check when your next Fastpass is available on the bottom of your latest Fastpass ticket.
10. Most rides do not offer Fastpasses from the beginning of the day until the park closes but rather only for a certain period of the day. The first Fastpass return times for attractions will be at least 30 minutes after park opening,

sometimes longer. In addition some attractions will not have Fastpass open towards the end of the day – this could be for the final 30 minutes, for the final two hours or longer. If you are unsure, ask the Cast Members at the attraction. Once all the day's Fastpasses have been used for an attraction, wait times will drop significantly.
11. The 'Indiana Jones' and 'Star Tours' Fastpasses are not linked with the rest of the system. This means you can hold a Fastpass for either of these two attractions AND another Disneyland Park attraction at the same time.

## Special Fastpass tickets:

Guests staying in Suites and State Club rooms at the Disneyland Hotel, Newport Bay Hotel, Hotel New York and Sequoia Lodge Hotel get one VIP Fastpass per guest. A VIP Fastpass offers instant entry through the Fastpass line of every attraction as many times of you want. This means that you will not need to use the standard Fastpass system with return times but rather instead you simply show the VIP Fastpass at the entry to each Fastpass-enabled ride to access the Fastpass queue line. You must still wait in all the standard queue lines at non-Fastpass enabled attractions.

Guests of the Disneyland Hotel not staying in suites or State Club rooms are given one Hotel Fastpass per person per day. This enables guests to access one Fastpass attraction per day through the Fastpass line immediately. After this voucher has been given to the ride attendant you will need to use the normal Fastpass system for the rest of the day. The Disneyland Hotel Fastpass is valid all day except between 1:00pm and 4:00pm.

**Chapter 10**
# Disney Village

Disney Village is an entertainment district located just next to the theme parks where you can continue the fun late into the night after the parks close. This area houses a theatre show, a cinema multiplex, restaurants, shops, bars and cafes and is free admission.

## Entertainment:
### Buffalo Bill's Wild West Show:

Located at the entrance to Disney Village, Buffalo Bill's is a dinner show staring Mickey and the gang as they venture through the Wild West.

The show is a fantastic way to spend an evening at Disneyland, combining live entertainment and a meal in one place. When looking at the price it is easy to criticize it – category one seating is priced at £63/€75, and category two seating is £51/€60 per adult. Children's prices are approximately £11/€13 less per person. These are expensive prices. However, when you compare the cost of the show to a visit to the theatre it becomes a lot easier to see the value – particularly as you get a meal included in the price, and a souvenir cowboy hat. Specially priced tickets for Mondays, Tuesdays and Wednesdays are available on the French www.disneylandparis.fr website for €37 to €42.

109

Category 2 seats are located further away from the action than Category 1 seats. Category 1 seating also includes a non-alcoholic welcome cocktail, and some treats with your tea or coffee during the dessert portion of your meal.

The adult menu is subject to change but generally includes cornbread, chili, skillet, corn on the cob with potato wedges, apple and ice-cream dessert, a drink (alcoholic [beer only] or not) with refills, and tea or coffee. As for the main course you can expect a roast chicken drumstick, sausage, potato wedges, ice cream and a drink. There is a separate kids menu too. All the food and drinks are included in the price and is served family-style.

The show itself is 90 minutes and features live animals, Mickey and Minnie (and friends), some incredible stunts and some great sets!

Special money saving tip: If you book the Wild West Show as part of your Disney package you will save 10% per person. This offer is available from 3rd April 2014 to 31$^{st}$ March 2015 (Excluding 25$^{th}$ to 30$^{th}$ December 2014).

There are two showings per night - at 6:30pm and 9:30pm – and the show only operates on select days every week.

If you are allergic to dust or animals, do not attend this show. Access to minors (under 18) is not permitted unless they are accompanied by an adult. Alcohol will only be served for guests aged 18 or over – ID may be required.

## Panoramagique:

Soar up into the sky and get a bird's-eye view of Disneyland Paris from the world's largest helium-filled passenger balloon – Panoramagique. This is a great way to get some aerial photos of the resort where you can clearly see all the land around you, including both theme parks, Disney Village and the resort hotels.

Pricing is €12 per adult and €6 per child for the flight. A meal deal which includes a flight on Panoramagique and a meal at the Earl of Sandwich is also available.

Note that flights will not operate in periods of high wind, or adverse weather conditions.

## Sports Bar:
Just because you are at Disneyland Paris does not mean you have to miss out on the latest in sporting action. Bring your friends and family down to the Sports Bar and watch the game on the big, big screen whilst having a drink or two and a snack. The Sports Bar also hosts weekly karaoke sessions and other forms of live entertainment open to all at no cost.

## Billy Bob's:
As well as being a restaurant during the day – more on this later in this section – Billy Bob's turns into a bar and nightclub as the night draws in. Due to it being at Disneyland Paris, children are allowed in at all times of the day and night. The bar is often frequented by Cast Members at the end of a hard day's work in the parks – here drinks are free-flowing and adults and children alike can dance the night away.

## Cinema Gaumont:
If you fancy catching a film, Disney Village's Gaumont cinema could be just the right place. With 15 different auditoriums, including one with an IMAX screen, there is bound to be something for you and your family to enjoy.

You can check film times in advance at http://www.cinemasgaumontpathe.com/cinemas/cinema-gaumont-disney-village/ - films tagged with "VF" are dubbed in French, "VO" are projected in their original language, and "VOST" are shown in their original language but with French subtitles added. Almost all films will be in French with one or two in their original language.

## Games Arcade:
Located by the Sports Bar, here you can choose from a series of classic arcade-style video games. Games are priced at €2 each.

## La Marina:
Fancy a unique way of travelling around Lake Disney? "La Marina" offers several different water activities for guests of all ages. From rowing boats to pedal boats, to electric boats and hydro bikes there is something for everyone. These water activities are available at a charge and operate based on weather conditions. Non-water based activities are also available including a mini train which drives around the lake, and the surrey bikes which you can roam freely on. Operating times are 4:00pm to 10:00pm daily during high season (school holidays) and on weekends based on the meteorological

conditions. Activities may also be available outside these times, based on attendance.

**Pricing:**
Electric boat hire - €20 for 20 minutes, 5 people maximum per boat
Hydro Bikes - €5 for 20 minutes, 1 person per bike. Minimum age: 12 years old
Pedal Boats - €10 for 20 minutes, 5 people maximum per boat.
Surrey bike - €10 for 20 minutes for a 2-adult + 1 child bike, or €15 for 20 minutes for a 4-adult + 1 child bike.
Mini train - €2 per person with stops at the Newport Bay Club Hotel, Sequoia Lodge Hotel and in front of Panoramagique.

# Restaurants:

**McDonald's** – Quick service location. McDonald's is a well known fast food joint worldwide. This location has bumped up its prices slightly. A standard meal costs between €8 and €9, with a child's meal costing about €5. If you are going to visit this location be aware that queues can be long if you do not use the automated terminals and want to order from an employee instead.

**Starbucks Coffee** – Quick service location. This is standard Starbucks location but it should be noted that Starbucks is not cheap in France and this location is no different. A hot or cold brewed drink is priced at between €4 and €6, and sandwiches are approximately €5 each.

**Earl of Sandwich** – Quick service location. Prices are about €7 for a "gourmet" heated sandwich, and €8 for a salad. The adult sandwich menu is priced at €11, with a kids' menu priced at €7.50.

An "Adult Balloon Flight" meal is available at Earl of Sandwich for €18.50 and includes a warm sandwich, a packet of scripts, a soda or a bottle of water, a chocolate brownie or cookie, and one flight aboard Panoramagique. A "Child Balloon Flight" meals is available for €10.50 and includes a mini-sandwich, a soda or bottle of water or Caprisun, a mini chocolate brownie or fruit cup, and one flight aboard Panoramagique.

**Cafe Mickey** - Character table service restaurant. Breakfast (at 8:00am and 9:30am daily) is priced at €25 for non-Disney hotel guests and €17 (£14) for Disney hotel guests as an upgrade to regular breakfast. Adult lunch and dinner set menus are priced at €36.50 (£33) without a drink. The children's menu is priced at €20.50 (£17) including one drink. Main courses priced €17 to €28 if purchased a la carte. Adult and children set menus are both included in the Plus Meal Plan. This meal can be pre-paid and pre-booked if booking a package through Disneyland Paris directly.

**Annette's Diner** – Table service restaurant. Breakfast menu priced at €11.50, There are several set menus priced at €19.50, €27 and €32. Children's set menu priced at €15. Main courses priced between €14 and €25 a la carte. Milkshakes priced at €7.50-€8.50. A take-away menu is also available priced at €16. The children's set menu and €32 adult set menu are both included in the Plus Meal Plan.

**King Ludwig's Castle** – Table service restaurant. There is a special lunch menu (dish of the day style) served until 3:00pm priced at €14. There are also three-course menus priced between €22 and €26 with no drinks. Main courses are priced between €16 and €27 a la carte.

**Planet Hollywood** – Table service restaurant. Main courses are priced between €15 and €33. Kids' menu priced at €12.50.

**Rainforest Cafe** - Table service restaurant. Adult set menu priced at €23.50; children's set menu priced at €14. Main courses are also available a la carte – salads are €18 to €19, burgers are priced at €19 to €25, pasta is €19.50 to €21, other main courses are priced at €22 to €33.

**The Steakhouse** – Table service restaurant. Set menus priced at €28, €33 and €40. A la Carte menu items are priced between €20 and €60. The children's menu is priced at €16. The children's set menu and €33 adult set menu are both included in the Plus Meal Plan.

**New York Style Sandwiches** - Counter service and snack location. The sandwich menu is priced at €14. Pizzas are priced at €11, the salad bar is priced between €7 and €9, pasta is priced at €9, sandwiches are priced at €6.50-€7. The children's menu is available for €8. This location also serves hot and cold drinks, and ice creams.

**Billy Bob's Country Western Saloon** – Billy Bob's is divided into two dining establishments – "Bar Snacks" which is a snack and quick service location, and "La Grange" which is an all you can eat Tex Mex buffet restaurant. Bar snacks menu priced at €14 for adults and €8 for children. A la carte items are priced between €2.50 and €9.50. The La Grange buffet costs €27 per adult (no drinks included) or €30.50 with one drink, and €14.50 per child with one drink included. The adult buffet with one drink, and the children's buffet are both included in the standard meal plan.

**Sports Bar** – Counter service and snack location. Snacks are served until 11:00pm. Sandwiches and burgers are priced between €9 and €11. Other selected warm dishes include pasta bolognaise, hot dogs and fish and chips priced between €8 and €11. Pizzas priced at €12 to €14 are also available. An adult sports bar menu is available for €14, along with a children's menu priced at €8.

# Shops:
After a meal in one of the many restaurants in the Disney Village you might want to treat yourself with a little bit of retail therapy, and here you are spoilt for choice with several merchandise locations.

**World of Disney** – As you walk into Disney Village from the parks this is the first store you will encounter. The "World Of Disney" store was unveiled in Summer 2012 and is the number one place to get your Disney merchandise outside of the parks. It is also the largest store at the entire resort featuring a beautiful interior, plenty of tills to pay at, and a good selection of merchandise.

**The Disney Store** – This classic location is like a traditional Disney store and has become slightly redundant since the opening of World of Disney. Here you can create your own lightsabers, and your own Mr. Potatohead figure, as well as purchase from a selection of more common merchandise.

**Planet Hollywood Store** – Get items with the Planet Hollywood brand on them. This store mainly stocks clothes.

**The Disney Gallery** – This location features collector's items such as figurines and paintings. In addition you can take advantage of Disney's 'Art on Demand' kiosks where you can order a poster from an interactive display. This poster will then be created to your specifications and delivered to your home – with over 200 different posters to choose from, there is bound to be something for everyone.

**LEGO Store** – This is the largest LEGO store in Europe, and a relatively new addition to Disney Village having been unveiled in March 2014. It features all kinds of different LEGO sets but unfortunately it does not feature any exclusive Disney-themed merchandise. Nevertheless, it is worth a visit.

**Disney Fashion** – For fans of Disney clothing, here is whether you will find your haven.

**World of Toys** – Despite its name, this store seems to mainly target girls and is *the* place to buy princess dresses, dolls, as well as sweets.

**Rainforest Café Store** – The perfect place to get all your Rainforest Café branded merchandise.

**Chapter 11**
# Touring Plans

Touring plans are easy to follow instructions that are designed to minimise your waiting time in queue lines throughout the day. By doing this you can maximise your time in the park to do many more attractions in the same day. There are several different touring plans available to suit your needs.

In order to see all of Disneyland Park you will need to allow at least two days – you will be able to hit the headliner attractions at the park in just one day, however, if you are pressed for time. Walt Disney Studios Park can be seen in one day. Unless you are going during a very quiet time of the year, you will be hard pressed to visit both parks and do the best rides of each in one day – there is simply not enough time.

These touring plans are definitely not set in stone so feel free to adapt them to suit the needs of your party. It is important to note that these plans focus on experiencing the rides; if your focus is on meeting the characters then a touring plan is not suitable for you as there is no way of minimising waits for characters, apart from the obvious tip of getting to the parks early.

These touring plans are intense, and you may very well be tired by the end of them BUT you will get to cram in as much as possible during your visit. If you are at the resort for multiple days feel free to follow the plans at a more leisurely pace. In addition, if you do not want to experience a particular ride, simply skip that step but do not change the order.

**Insider Tip:** In order to minimise the time you spend waiting in queue lines, you will often need to cross the park from one side to the other – this is purposely done by theme parks to disperse crowds more evenly. Note for example how the three rollercoasters at Disneyland Park are all in different lands and far away from each other – the same also applies at Walt Disney Studios Park.

# Disneyland Park:
## 1 Day Plan for Guests using Extra Magic Hours:
**Step 1**: At 7:50am be at the park gates for entry. At 8:00am, the park will open. Make sure you pick up both a Park Guide and a Times Guide under the archways of Main Street USA Station. These will tell you parade, show and firework times, as well as attraction closures. Walk down Main Street USA, get photos and proceed straight to Sleeping Beauty Castle.

**Step 2**: - Decide whether you want to prioritise thrill rides or kids rides. If you want thrills enter Discoveryland and ride *Space Mountain: Mission 2*, followed by *Buzz Lightyear Laser Blast*. If you want rides focused towards children enter Fantasyland and ride to *Dumbo the Flying Elephant* first, followed by *Peter Pan's Flight*.

**Step 3**: As long as you arrived at the park for opening and Extra Magic Hours are running for two hours, it should now be 8:45am at the very latest, and you have plenty of time to do other attractions. Although there is not a specific list of rides that Disneyland Paris guarantees will be open for this morning period you will still have enough time to experience the following attractions provided they are open: *Mad Hatter's Tea Cups, Le Carrousel de Lancelot* and *Orbitron: Machines Volantes*. On most days, unless attendance is exceptionally high, you should easily be able to do all of these Extra Magic Hours rides before the rest of the park opens at 10:00am.

**Step 4**: By 9:50am make sure to make your way back to the park's hub in front of the castle. Here you will stand behind the rope at the entrance to Frontierland along with other guests.

**Step 5**: At 10:00am when the park opens go directly to *Big Thunder Mountain*. Ride it.

**Step 6**: Now it is decision time again – What do you fancy doing? A) Driving a car or B) Meeting the Disney Princesses. If you fancy driving a car, walk over to *Autopia* in Discoveryland. Otherwise you can go to *Princess Pavilion* in Fantasyland. Queues for both these attractions get very, very long throughout the day. At certain times of the year *Princess Pavilion* operates a ticketed system – see the Disneyland Park chapter of this guide for more information on this.

**Step 7**: Next decision: Do you fancy meeting Mickey Mouse or a ride into outer space? *Meet Mickey Mouse* in Fantasyland is the permanent home for the big cheese himself. Or for the space adventurers it is time to ride *Star Tours* in Discoveryland.

**Step 8**: At this point, you have been made to make a lot of decisions, but now is your chance to do any rides you have opted not to do so far. If, for example, you opted to go to *Autopia* and *Star Tours*, then now is the time to *Meet Mickey Mouse* and *Princess Pavilion* (and vice-versa). Lines for these attractions will only continue to increase into the evening hours, plus meet and greet locations shut several hours before the park closes.

**Step 9:** It should now be time to grab some lunch.

**Step 10:** You now have a few rides left to do in Fantasyland. Now is the time to experience: *Casey Junior*, *Le Pays des Contes de Fees (Storybook Canal Boats)*, *Snow White* and *Pinocchio*. Ride these one after another, in this order if you want to do them all. *Casey Junior* and *Storybook* will close at least three hours before the rest of the park.

**Step 11:** Watch *Captain EO* in Discoveryland.

**Step 12**: Parade time - Is it time for the Parade yet? Grab a spot on Main Street USA at least 30 minutes before *Disney Magic on Parade*. The parade is traditionally between 5:00pm and 7:00pm but make sure to check your "Times Guide" for more information and exact times. Show up 45 minutes before or even earlier if you want a particularly good spot.

**Step 13:** A huge number of people exit the park after the parade so the park will begin to become less busy. Now is the time to either take a bit of a rest and relax or go to the rides that have fast moving queues. Ride *Pirates of the Caribbean*.

**Step 13**: Ride *its a small world*. This is another attraction which handles thousands of guests an hour so queues are always moving.

**Step 14**: Ride *Indiana Jones et le Temple du Peril*

**Step 16**: Head to *Phantom Manor*. Do not forget to explore the graveyard section located by the ride exit for some great puns!

**Step 17**: Check what time the nighttime show *Disney Dreams* is being performed. This is a show which is not to be missed. Now depending on what time of the day it is, and when the park closes, it is either time to go and watch *Disney Dreams*, have dinner or go and do the walkthrough attractions. Walkthrough attractions do not have a waiting time. These include: *Adventure Isle* and *La Cabane des Robinson*, *Le Passage Enchante d'Aladdin*, *Alice's Curious Labyrinth*, and the wonderfully themed *Les Mysteres de Nautilus*.
**Step 18**: Get a spot in front of the castle or on Main Street USA 30 to 60 minutes before *Disney Dreams*. See our section on Disney Dreams for help finding the perfect spot. We recommend grabbing a hot dog from Casey's Corner to eat whilst waiting to help the time pass.

## 1 Day Plan with No Extra Magic Hours – Focus on: kids rides and experiences:

**Step 1** - Arrive at 9:20am at Disneyland Park's entrance. Enter as the park pre-opens at 9:30am – from this time until 10:00am you are able to shop and eat on Main Street USA as well as ride the Main Street vehicles. Make sure you pick up both a Park Guide and a Times Guide under the archways of Main Street USA Station. These will tell you parade, show, charater and firework times, as well as attraction closures and park opening hours. Walk down Main Street USA, get photos and proceed straight to Sleeping Beauty Castle. At Sleeping Beauty Castle's hub lies the entrance to all the lands of the park – Fantasyland and Discoveryland will be open to Disney Hotel guests and some Annual Passholders at this time. Otherwise, the lands will be cordoned off. Stand by the rope leading to the castle. This rope will be removed at 10:00am allowing all guests to go through.
**Step 2** – As you cross and go through the castle entrance, you now enter Fantasyland. Go to *Dumbo: The Flying Elephant*. Ride this attraction – it will have significant queues later in the day.
**Step 3** - Go to *Princess Pavilion*. Meet one of the Princesses here.
**Step 4** - Obtain a *Peter Pan's Flight* Fastpass.
**Step 5** - Go to *Meet Mickey Mouse*. Meet Mickey at this attraction.
**Step 6** - Go to *Casey Junior*. Ride this attraction.

**Step 7** – Just next door is *Le Pays des Contes de Fees*. Ride it.
**Step 8** – It should now be time to have lunch.
**Step 9** - Use your *Peter Pan's Flight* Fastpass.
**Step 10** - Get a *Buzz Lightyear Laser Blast* Fastpass from Discoveryland
**Step 11** - Ride *Pinocchio*, and *Snow White's Scary Adventures* (located next to each other) in Fantasyland.
**Step 12** - Watch *Captain EO* in Discoveryland.
**Step 13** – Use your *Buzz Lightyear Laser Blast* Fastpass.
**Step 14** - Get a spot at least 45 minutes before the beginning of *Disney Magic on Parade* on Main Street USA or anywhere else along the parade route. The parade is traditionally between 5:00pm and 7:00pm but make sure to check your "Times Guide" for more information and exact times.
**Step 15** - Ride *Autopia* and/or explore inside *Sleeping Beauty Castle*. If you still have a lot of time left until the park closes, do both attractions.
**Step 16** - Ride *it's a small world* in Fantasyland.
**Step 17** - Decision: Explore *Alice's Curious Labyrinth* or ride *Le Carousel de Lancelot*. If you still have a lot of time left until the park closes, do both attractions.
**Step 18** - Ride *Pirates of the Caribbean* in Adventureland.
**Step 19** - Ride *Phantom Manor* in Frontierland.
**Step 20** – Have dinner and watch *Disney Dreams*. Get a spot in front of the castle or on Main Street USA 30 to 60 minutes before *Disney Dreams*. See our section on Disney Dreams for help finding the perfect spot. We recommend grabbing a hot dog from Casey's Corner to eat whilst waiting to help the time pass.

Note that if your children want a bit of a thrill and want to ride a coaster, *Big Thunder Mountain* in Frontierland should be your choice. You should get a Fastpass for this after the *Buzz Lightyear's Laser Blast* Fastpass.

## 1 Day Plan with No Extra Magic Hours – Focus on: Thrill rides and experiences:

**Step 1** - Arrive at 9:20am at the entrance to Disneyland Park. Enter as the park pre-opens at 9:30am – from this time until 10:00am you are able to shop and eat on Main Street USA as well as ride the Main Street vehicles. Make sure you pick up both a Park Guide and a Times Guide under the archways of Main Street USA Station. These will tell you parade, show and firework times, as well as attraction closures. Walk down Main Street USA, get photos and proceed straight to Sleeping Beauty Castle. At Sleeping Beauty Castle's hub lies the entrance to all the lands of the park – Fantasyland and Discoveryland will be open to Disney Hotel guests and some Annual Pass Holders. Otherwise, the lands will be cordoned off, stand by the rope leading to the castle. This rope will be removed at 10:00am allowing all guests to go through.

**Step 2** - Go to *Big Thunder Mountain Railroad* in Frontierland immediately as the park opens. Ride it.

**Step 3** - Go to *Space Mountain: Mission 2* in Discoveryland. Ride it.

**Step 4** - Go to *Star Tours*. Ride this attraction.

**Step 5** - Go to *Indiana Jones et le Temple du Peril* in Adventureland. Ride it. By this time, you will have ridden all the rollercoasters in this park.

**Step 6** - Go to *Pirates of the Caribbean*. Ride this attraction.

**Step 7** - Go to Discoveryland. Get a *Buzz Lightyear Laser Blast* FastPass.

**Step 8** – It should now be time to have lunch.

**Step 9** - Ride *Autopia*.

**Step 10** - Go and watch *Captain EO: Starring Michael Jackson*.

**Step 11** - If it is time for your *Buzz Lightyear Laser Blast* Fastpass, use it or skip to step 12.

**Step 12** - Ride *it's a small world*

**Step 13** - Get *Peter Pan's Flight* Fastpass.

**Step 14** - Use your *Buzz Lightyear Laser Blast* Fastpass if it still has not been used.

**Step 15** - Get a spot at least 45 minutes before the beginning of *Disney Magic on Parade* on Main Street USA or anywhere else along the parade route. The parade is traditionally between 5:00pm and 7:00pm but make sure to check your "Times Guide" for more information and exact times.
**Step 16** - Ride *Phantom Manor*
**Step 17** - Explore *Les Mysteres de Nautilus* and other walk-through areas such as *Le Pasage Enchante d'Aladdin*.
**Step 18** – Use your *Peter Pan's Flight* FastPass and explore *Alice's Curious Labyrinth*.
**Step 19** – Have dinner
**Step 20** - Get a spot in front of the castle or on Main Street USA 30 to 60 minutes before *Disney Dreams*. See our section on Disney Dreams for help finding the perfect spot. We recommend grabbing a hot dog from Casey's Corner to eat whilst waiting to help the time pass.


Notes:
- The attractions that are missed in these touring plans are: *Thunder Mesa Riverboat Landing* (The wait time is never longer than 30 minutes so you may be able to fit it in) and the *Disneyland Railroad* which goes around the park (queues are shortest at the Frontierland station, feel free to do this whenever you want. There are stations in 4 different places around the park, see the park map).
- Disneyland Paris also lists the following as attractions so you might want to fit them in at some point: *Horse-Drawn Streetcars* (Main Street USA – enjoyable but walking is quicker), *Main Street Vehicles* (same as before) and the *Liberty* and *Discovery Arcades* (indoor shopping areas filled with details).
- This guide does not take into account any live shows as those vary throughout the year, check your "Times Guide" for more. Make sure to go and watch them.
- Also make sure to visit the Gallery inside Sleeping Beauty castle (upstairs) and the Dragon's Lair underneath. Entry to Sleeping Beauty Castle closes at least one hour before

*Disney Dreams*, as does the whole of Fantasyland.
- You will not be able to do all the attractions in the park in one day (without Extra Magic Hours and some luck) unless the park is exceptionally quiet with a very low number of visitors. Note that there are several choices to be made throughout the day so you will have to be selective.
- You must already have your tickets purchased and in hand to make the most of your time and these touring plans. If you still need to buy them (why would you when they are cheaper in advance?), turn up at least 30 minutes earlier than the start times recommended on these plans. You will need to be there even earlier during peak season to buy tickets.

# Walt Disney Studios Park:
## The definitive touring plan:
**Step 1** - Arrive at 9:20am at the Walt Disney Studios Park entrance. Enter the park at 9:30am when it pre-opens. Get a Park Map and a Times Guide as you enter Studio 1. Walk through Studio 1 briskly and do not waste time admiring it – you can do that later.

**Step 2** - When you come out of the other side of Studio 1, turn right after the statue of Mickey and Walt Disney and walk past *The Art of Disney Animation* and *Animagique* towards the *Flying Carpets over Agrabah*. To the left of *Flying Carpets over Agrabah* is *Crush's Coaster*. Form a queue outside the "Wait time" sign or join the one that is already there. They will usually start letting guests in just before 10:00am.

**Step 3** – Pick up a Fastpass for *Ratatouille: The Adventure as Fastpasses for this ride are distributed very quickly.*

**Step 4** - Visit *Toy Story Playland*. There are several attractions to experience here. Ride them in this order: *Toy Soldiers Parachute Drop, Slinky Dog, RC Racer*.

**Step 5** - Ride *Cars Quatre Roues Rallye* – this is located opposite *Crush's Coaster*.

**Step 6** - Ride *Rock n' Rollercoaster*.

**Step 7** - Experience *Armageddon*.

**Step 8** – Hopefully at least two hours will have elapsed since you picked up your Fastpass for *Ratatouille: The Adventure,* so go and pick up a Fastpass for *Tower of Terror*.
**Step 9** – Fit lunch in around your Fastpass time for *Ratatouille: The Adventure*, if it is time to ride the attraction now do so first. If not, have lunch and return to use your Fastpass.
**Step 10** - Ride *Studio Tram Tour*.
**Step 11** - Ride *Flying Carpets over Agrabah*.
**Step 12** – Use your *Tower of Terror* Fastpass if it is time. If it is not, then skip forward to step 13 and fit *Tower of Terror* in around the show times.
**Step 13** – That is it for all the rides. This park is tiny in comparison with Disneyland Park! Now there are five main attractions left to experience – all are shows, so take these in according to their schedules which are available outside the attractions themselves and in the Times Guide which you picked up earlier. These shows are:

- *Lights, Motors, Action*
- *Stitch Live*
- *Disney Junior Live*
- *Animagique*
- *Cinemagique*

Chapter 12
# Outside The Parks

A trip to Disneyland Paris does not have to stop at the resort. After all, you are near one of Europe's largest and most vibrant cities, plus there are opportunities for shopping and much more nearby.

## Paris:

Disneyland Paris is located a mere 35 minutes away from the centre of Paris by train so visiting the 'City Of Lights' is a must-do on a multiple day trip.

Paris is filled with monuments, museums and rich culture and history. You should make sure to visit the following world class attractions during your trip to the city: the Eiffel Tower, the Louvre museum, Musee d'Orsay, Arc de Triumph, Champs Elysees, Notre Dame, Montmartre and the Sacre Coeur. Fans of churches will be delighted by Paris' varied collection. Museums are generally reasonably priced, and European Economic Area citizens aged under 26 get free entry to most museums in the city. In addition non-EEA visitors under the age of 18 get free entry with proof. There are even monthly openings of the museums where everyone can get free admission, regardless of age.

We also recommend taking in a river cruise on The Seine or a bus tour which will allow you to see many of these monuments from the exterior in one go.

If you are planning on visiting a lot of paid-admission attractions, and fancy a bus tour and unlimited transport, the Paris Pass could be the perfect option for you. It is available at www.independentguidebooks.com/parispass.

For those who fancy travelling to Paris by arranging their own transport, we recommend catching the regional RER A train towards the centre of Paris from Marne-la-Vallee – Chessy station. Once you are in the centre of Paris you may need to use the metro to get to various destinations. A Mobilis day pass is the best option and is priced at €16.10 per adult for the zones required (zones 1-5) and allows you travel all day until midnight on Paris' transport system.

## Paris Excursions

Disneyland Paris runs daily excursions to the city of Paris so you can see the sights without any of the hassle of planning it yourself. They run two excursions:

**Magical Day Tour of Paris** - Transport is by coach with individual headsets detailing fun facts, as well as history and culture in English. You will visit the second floor of the Eiffel Tower or visit the Louvre. You will also cruise along the Seine and see the sights. From 13th November 2014 to 31st March 2015 the price is £68 (€83) per adult and £42 (€52) per child. Prices from 1st April 2015 to 23rd March 2016 are £74 per adult and £49 per child. The bus departs from the Hotel New York at 9:45am and returns at approximately 6:30pm.

**Paris Essentials** - This is a more free-style tour where you get time to explore for yourself. It includes a return coach trip from Disneyland Paris area hotels and an open-top sightseeing bus tour in the city centre. From 13th November 2014 to 31st March 2015 the price is £46 (€57) per adult and £31 (€38) per child. Prices from 1st April 2015 to 23rd March 2016 are £47 per adult and £31 per child. The coach departs from three locations: Newport Bay Club hotel, Vienna International Magic circus hotel and Hotel l'Elysee Val d'Europe between 10:15am and 10:40am depending on which hotel you are at. The return time will be at about 7:00pm.

# Val d' Europe:

Located just two minutes away from Disneyland Paris, you can also visit the town of Val d' Europe, which is only one stop away on the RER train (about €1.80 per journey or the number 50 bus which is free from just outside Marne la Vallee - Chessy train station).

Val d'Europe houses one of the largest shopping centres in Europe! If you would like to stock up on groceries, there is a hypermarket in the centre, as well as SeaLife centre aquarium (entry is about €10 per person), and many other stores. Outside you will find the 'La Vallee Village' outlets which feature designer luxury goods at reduced prices.

## Davy Crockett's Adventure:
If you like adventure assault courses, you will love this! There are swings, trapezes, rope bridges, ladders and much more for you to explore making this amazing family fun. This attraction is located at the Davy Crockett Ranch – a campsite run by Disneyland Paris and considered to be one of the seven on-site hotels, despite being located 8km from the main resort hub.

This activity is open seasonally – you should call the Disneyland Paris reservation line for specific opening times for this attraction or visit http://www.aventure-aventure.com (French only). Note there is no shuttle bus to the Davy Crockett Campsite where this activity is located, so you will need a car if you wish to participate in the adventure, or alternatively book a taxi.

## Golf Disneyland:
Golf Disneyland is a world-class 27-hole golf course located right on Disneyland Paris property and open to all visitors, including hotel and day guests. You can rent out golf equipment and have a go yourself or watch others play. Visitor green fees for 18 holes start at approximately €50 per person on weekdays and €75 on weekends. 9 holes cost €35 and €45 respectively. A reduced rate for the 18-hole course is available for those aged under 25 years old.

The golf course is open year-round, except on Christmas Day and New Year's Day. Club rentals are €27 for a complete set, or €5 per club. There is a restaurant and bar overlooking the course and golf cart hire is available too. The Pro Shop is also on site, which sells a large variety of golfing gear. Lessons are also available. To make a reservation you can email dlp.golf.disneyland@disney.com or call +33 (0) 1 60 45 68 90.

Chapter 13
# Guests with Disabilities:

Disneyland Paris is a place designed to be enjoyed by everyone, regardless of their mental or physical abilities. Unlike many buildings, forms of transport and even cities around the world, Disneyland Paris was built with accessibility in mind – even including something as simple as making sure that there are no steps from hotel rooms to any theme park attraction as the whole resort was built on one flat level.

When it comes to theme parks and attractions, Disney is undoubtedly one of the industry leaders in making accommodations for its guests. At Disneyland Paris alone, over 60,000 disabled people visit the resort every year. This chapter aims to give you a general outline of what services and facilities are available to disabled guests, as well as other guests such as pregnant mothers and guests with temporary disabilities.

## Accessibility Cards:

All parties of guests with disabilities should make sure to stop by Guest Relations at either park on the first day of their visit. In Disneyland Park this is City Hall (on the left after the train station) and at Walt Disney Studios Park this is at Studio Services (on the right in the entrance plaza area before entering Studio 1).

At guest relations, guests who have a disability, and expectant mothers, can apply for one of two cards that will facilitate their visit and entry into attractions - the Priority Card and the Easy Access Card.

The **Priority Card** allows a disabled guest and up to 4 members of their party access to an attraction via a specially adapted entrance. This entrance will involve less walking and no stairs to navigate. It could be through the ride's exit, through the Fastpass entrance or through a specially adapted queue line – it could also be that the standard queue line is adapted and therefore you will use that one. Entry procedures vary from ride to ride – to learn what boarding options are available to you at each attraction simply ask the Cast Member at the entrance to each of these.

This is not instant access and wait times vary based on the number of people in the Priority Card queue at the time. In order to receive the card, the disabled person (or their helper) must present supporting documents or a medical certificate. Proof of ID is also required and may be asked for by a Cast Member when boarding a ride to prove authenticity.

Supporting documentation to prove disability for guests from France includes one of the following: disability card, disabled person's priority card, difficulty standing card, war disability card or European disabled parking badge. For guests from outside France the following are accepted: disability card, European disabled parking badge or a medical certificate (stating that the person has a disability in French or English, signed and stamped by a doctor and issued within the last 3 months).

The **Easy Access Card** is not designed for disabled guests but rather for those with temporary or debilitating illnesses or injuries (that have not led to them being registered as disabled). The Easy Access Card is also available for expectant mothers. It acts in the same way as the Priority Card, giving you access via a specially adapted entrance - this card does not, however, offer priority access. A medical certificate is required for this card. This certificate must state that the person has a debilitating illness, is temporary disabled or is pregnant in French or English, signed and stamped by a doctor and issued within the last 3 months. Only one helper may accompany the disabled guest on attractions, unless they have a "carte de priorité familiale" in which case all helpers named on this card may also board with the disabled person.

Some attractions will require people with these disability cards (and with certain disabilities) to make a reservation and return later, instead of waiting in line. It is usually possible to repeat an attraction after you have experienced it provided you exit and return a few minutes later.

## Hearing-impaired visitors:
The Disney Parks information points as well as some Walt Disney Studios Park attractions are equipped with induction loops to assist guests. These attractions are: *CinéMagique, Animagique, Disney Junior Live on Stage!, Stitch Live!* and *The Twilight Zone: Tower of Terror*. Other attractions do not require audio for full enjoyment.

## Mobility impaired visitors:
- Cast Members cannot escort or help disabled guests get to the different attractions. They will of course provide directions and help inside attractions.
- Some attractions require that disabled guests move their wheelchair to an attraction vehicle. For these attractions, disabled guests must be accompanied by at least one able-bodied adult (at least 18 years of age) to assist. Cast Members are not permitted to help visitors get out of their wheelchair. For some attractions, visitors must be able to move independently and climb stairs.
- In Walt Disney Studios Park, the queues for all attractions are wheelchair accessible; this is also the case for some attractions in Disneyland Park (Buzz Lightyear Laser Blast, Princess Pavilion and Meet Mickey Mouse). For attractions where this is not the case, a Priority Card (mentioned above in this section) allows guests entry via a separate specially designated entrance.
- A designated viewing area for guests in wheelchairs is available for the parade and also for certain shows.
- All toilets have accessible areas for visitors with reduced mobility.
- Companion toilets (which are also accessible) are available in every land of Disneyland Park. These toilets are also available at *Moteurs... Action ! Stunt Show Spectacular* in Walt Disney Studios Park during performances.
- All shops and table service restaurants are fully accessible. In quick service restaurants if help is needed, do not hesitate to contact a Cast Member for assistance.
- An accessible shuttle bus between all Disney hotels (except Davy Crockett Ranch) and the theme parks is available. Simply ask at the hotel desk, the Disney Express desk in Marne La Vallee – Chessy station, or guest services in the parks for details and to book their complimentary service.

- In the hotels there are several rooms adapted to meet the needs of those in wheelchairs. Each room has an extra-large bathroom with a bath, handrails and raised toilet. Connecting rooms are available if required. Additionally, mobility-impaired guests can hire a special seat that enables them to wash without assistance (to be requested when making the reservation). The bedroom door is fitted with a spyhole positioned at wheelchair height in accessible rooms. Bathrooms at Disney's Davy Crockett Ranch, Disney's Sequoia Lodge and Disney's Santa Fe are fitted with a shower that is suitable for guests who are mobility impaired.

## Visually impaired guests:

- In some attractions, you will experience exactly the same sensations as other visitors. In others, you will need your companion to describe the surroundings.
- The Priority Card allows access to some attractions through special entrances for visually impaired visitors (see the Disney Parks Accessibility Guide for more information). Each attraction has its own access arrangements.
- At hotels, Disney recommends that visually impaired guests inform the hotel reception of their visual impairment as soon as they arrive. A Cast Member will be responsible for showing guests to their room, and showing them around the rest of the Disney hotel so that visually impaired guests can orientate themselves. Telephones and television remote controls with large buttons as well as room keys with braille are available on request. These can be requested when reserving a Disney Hotel room or at reception upon arrival.

### Guide dogs:

Guide and assistant dogs are allowed in the parks and on certain attractions. On attractions where they are not permitted, dogs must be left with another helper. They may not be left unattended or with a Cast Member at any time. Visually impaired guests may need to be accompanied on certain attractions, so if they plan on bringing a guide dog there must be at least three people in their group – the disabled person, someone to accompany the disabled person and a helper to take care of the guide dog

## Food allergies:
Disneyland Paris' food supplier offers several allergen free meals at selected restaurants. The best policy is to warn your hotel in advance so an allergen free breakfast can be prepared. Booking table service meals in advance and stating your allergies when making the reservation is also hugely beneficial. To view the range of options available at the resort make sure to review Disneyland Paris' allergen guide available online at http://www.disneylandparis.co.uk/content/GB/EN/Neutral/system/images/food_allergies.pdf

## Other important information:
- Note that Cast Members have the right to refuse you access to a particular attraction for your safety, or for any other reason.
- Some attractions only accept one disabled guest at once for safety reasons and because of French law. In these cases, waits for a disabled guest may be as long than the standard queue line.
- Read the safety instructions available at the entrance to every ride.
- The Disney Parks Accessibility Guide available online at http://www.disneylandparis.com/BROCHURE/handicap/uk/catalogue/files/html5/index.html?o=portrait is very useful and detailed - make sure to read it before leaving for your trip. It is also available at the parks at Guest Services.
- Medication that needs to be kept cool may be left at one of the First Aid points located in the two parks or in Disney Village.
- For safety reasons, all visitors: with reduced mobility or visual impairment, with a cognitive or mental health disorder, with behaviour disorder or autism or with a learning disability must be accompanied by at least one able-bodied companion over the age of 18 who can assist them. There is an exception for particular attractions that allow companions to accompany several persons with disabilities (see details for each attraction in the Disney Parks Accessibility Guide).
- Please note that some attractions may have low-light areas, flashing lights or loud sound effects, dropping floors and other effects. Companions should pay particular attention to all these factors when preparing for the stay and should read the safety information available at the entrance to each attraction.

Chapter 14
# Meeting The Characters

For some visitors, children or otherwise, meeting the characters is the highlight of their trip to Disneyland Paris. Being able to play games with Pluto, talk to Cinderella and hug Mickey always makes for moments that will last a lifetime.

The characters appear throughout the day in several locations including Disneyland Park, Walt Disney Studios Park, the hotels and in the Disney Village area.

## Disneyland Park:

The characters are scheduled to appear around the park at different times throughout the day. Mickey can be found in his "backstage" theatre area at Meet Mickey Mouse in Fantasyland and the princesses can be found at Princess Pavilion (also in Fantasyland). One character is also usually available to meet to the left of Casey's Corner – this character varies seasonally and in the past has been Winnie the Pooh, Minnie, Rapunzel and now even Merida. Many characters will make unannounced appearances throughout the parks too such as Darth Vader and The Seven Dwarves. If there is a specific character you would like to see, there is no harm asking at City Hall (to the left just before entering Main Street U.S.A.) and checking if they have a specific schedule for that character that has not been made publicly available. Not all characters will be available on all days, especially the more minor ones - they do need their days off after all.

You can also take part in a character dining experience at Auberge de Cendrillon where you can meet the Disney princesses as you dine (priced at about €66 [£55] per adult, €37 [£31] per child).

Finally there are the planned and scheduled meet and greets. Check your park times guide for these but they commonly include Winnie the Pooh, Donald Duck, Chip and Dale, Jack Sparrow and others.

## Walt Disney Studios Park:
You will find a lot of characters in the Toon Studio area of the park to the left of *Crush's Coaster* where there are permanent outdoor photo locations. Here you will often find Mickey, Minnie, Buzz Lightyear and other characters. Check your Times Guide for exact character appearances. In the afternoon you can often also find characters who were previously in the old Stars n' Cars parade in the park – you will usually see them by the stage area in front of Cinemagique.

*September 2014 update*: Since April 2014 guests have had the opportunity to meet and greet with Spider-Man himself in "Meet Spider-Man" located just opposite the entrance to Rock n' Rollercoaster at Walt Disney Studios Park. This has proved extremely popular with waits of up to 90 minutes to meet the character. Spider-Man was only scheduled to be at this location until July 2014 but this has been extended again and again. It is unclear whether Spiderman will be available to meet through the 2014 Halloween and Christmas seasons, and throughout 2015.

## Hotels:
Disneyland Paris no longer have characters at the hotels during breakfast, as these were removed in November 2014. There are now more characters in the parks in the morning instead.

However, Disneyland Hotel has characters dining options. For character dinners try Inventions in Disneyland Hotel (€60 adults, €30 kids). Inventions also hosts a brunch on Sundays (€64 adults, €32 kids, from 1:00 to 3:00pm) - you can participate in both of these even if you are not staying at the hotel.

## Disney Village:
You can meet the characters in Disney Village in two dining locations - Cafe Mickey and Buffalo Bill's Wild West Show.

Cafe Mickey serves breakfast, lunch and dinner and the characters rotate periodically but feature the main ones like Mickey Mouse, Pluto, Chip and Dale, Goofy and Minnie. Specific characters cannot be guaranteed as they change regularly throughout the day.

Buffalo Bill's Wild West Show - Here you will be able to get a photo with Mickey Mouse in his Wild West costume before every show. You will need to be there early as Mickey does head off early to prepare for the show. Admission into the show is required. Other characters participate in the show but are not available for meet and greets.

**Character Meeting Tips:**
1. *Meet Mickey Mouse* and the *Princess Pavilion* have organized queue areas with a waiting time posted by the entrance. Other characters that are present in the Times Guide will also have a queue formed with the help of Cast Members – here it will be hard to tell how long you will have to wait until you meet your characters. A good bet is about one minute per group ahead of you – some people will spend longer with the characters but most will average around one minute. When there are unscheduled character appearances most of these will involve a free-for-all queuing system – where this is no queue at all. Guests will crowd around the character and you will simply have to nudge yourself or your child forward in order for them to get a turn.
2. If your child has never met a character before, particularly the furry ones, it can be intimidating for them. Approach the character with your child slowly and never force a child and character to interact. As a former cast member, I have seen a lot of parents do this, hoping for a beautiful photo. Instead, they get a panicked child who breaks down into tears. Take the characters at the child's pace - some children love the characters, and others are terrified. Generally children are more accepting and willing to approach 'face' characters where a real human face is shown such as The Mad Hatter or the Princesses. It is understandable – sometimes a Mickey Mouse that is three times bigger than a child was not what they

were expecting, having only seen them on TV at home.
3. For any adults thinking of taking photos with the characters or getting autographs signed, it is completely fine, it is not frowned upon and the characters really like it as it allows them to have different interactions than with children.
4. Most characters are accompanied by a character-helper to keep them safe. Hand your camera or mobile phone to the character helper, ask them nicely and they will take a photo of you altogether if you would like.
5. Never injure a character, or pull on them or their costume – they have feelings too.
6. Characters will stay in role at all times – ask them about something from their movie and feel immersed in their world.
7. Some characters are silent – all 'fur' characters where you cannot see a performer's human face are not able to talk to you, no matter how hard you try.

Chapter 15
# Doing Disney on a budget

A visit to Disneyland Paris is pricey – it is priced as a premium luxury theme park destination and once you account for travel, park tickets, accommodation, food and souvenirs it is easy to see why for many families it is a once in a lifetime visit that they save a long time for. However, there are many ways of reducing your spending at the resort without compromising on the memories you will make.

## Traveling to Disneyland Paris:

**Drive** – Most of Disneyland Paris' visitors are located from across Europe making a trip by car feasible. For example, looking at travel from the UK to Disneyland Paris, if you are in the southeast of the UK, driving is usually a good option. This includes a ferry crossing or travel through the Eurotunnel. Both crossings are good value priced at about £50-£150 return when booked in advance for a car and all its passengers crossing from the UK to France. From Calais in France is it an easy three and a half hour drive. There are approximately €20 of toll roads each way from Calais to Disneyland Paris plus petrol costs.

**Budget and cheap flights** – Prices for budget flights can be appealing but beware of where these flights land. Prices can be as low as £20/€30 each way from across Europe to Paris. We recommend being especially wary of "Paris Beauvais-Tille Airport" which is actually located 120km away from Disneyland Paris – this is a drive of at least one and half hours from the airport to the parks. Shuttle services are also available but will cost about €200 for a return trip for a family of four. More information is available in Chapter 4: Getting there.

**Train** - Finally there are TGV and Eurostar trains to get you to the resort. If travelling from across France take a look at Ouigo (**http://www.ouigo.com**) which offers vastly discounted travel on TGV trains from selected locations across France. Otherwise, standard 'TGV Prems' fares booked in advance can be good value. You will want to arrive at *Marne la Vallee – Chessy* station.

For UK visitors Eurostar trains can be reasonably priced. If booked far enough in advance, you can get a return ticket from London to Disneyland Paris for £69 per person. For those who do not live in the capital, you can also book "through fares" which are one total fare from your local rail station at home to Disneyland Paris through the Eurostar website. You will need to change trains at St. Pancras. For example, through fares from Manchester to Paris are £90 per person. You will not need to pay for any airport transfers of course if you are using the Eurostar so factor that into your price comparisons.

# Planning:

1. **Disney Hotels** - Do you really need to stay at a Disney hotel? They are well themed and clean, but are very expensive compared to other local hotels. A nearby hotel such as the Kyriad has offers starting at €60 per night. See Chapter 5: The Hotels. Remember that a non-Disney hotel will not allow you to use Extra Magic Hours and you will have to buy your own park tickets separately.

2. **Buy an annual pass** - If you plan on visiting the theme parks for three or more days in a row, then buying an annual passport can work out cheaper than a three-day ticket and will get you discounts on food and merchandise.

3. **Wait for a special offer** – The marketing team at Disneyland Paris are always running a special offer of some sort, whether it is 25% off your trip, or kids go free, or an extra day and night free, there is never a reason to book without an offer. If there are no offers when you want to make your booking, wait a few days.

4. **Downgrade your hotel** - Do you really need a luxurious Disney hotel? Will you ever use the pool? If not, downgrade to somewhere like Disney's Hotel Cheyenne or Disney's Santa Fe Hotel. You will still get many of the same benefits such as Extra Magic Hours regardless of what hotel you stay in.

5. **Tickets** - If you are not staying at a Disney hotel, make sure to pre-purchase tickets. Buying them at the ticket booths on the day is expensive and time consuming. See Chapter 6: Tickets for more information on this.

6. **Visit during quieter times** - When the parks are less busy, you will be able to do more each day. Hotel prices are often cheaper too. Check out the When to visit section of this guide.

## At the Parks:

1. **Eat at the Disney Village** - Yes, it is not the healthiest option but there is a McDonald's at the Disney Village which sells fast-food at prices cheaper than food in the theme parks. Be prepared for long queues however. Or try, the healthier and equally well-priced Earl of Sandwich located next door.

2. **Meal vouchers** - If you want to eat at the theme park restaurants every day of your stay then pre-purchasing meal vouchers online or over the phone can save you money. They can added at the time of booking or anytime before your trip. These can only be added if you are staying at a Disney hotel and you must purchase them for the entire stay.

3. **Packed lunches** – To save money why not make your own packed lunches or save a few croissants from breakfast at your hotel (this is an ethical grey area). There is also a supermarket at the Marne-La-Vallee - Chessy train station that stocks essentials which you can take in the parks with you, or there is a huge supermarket called Auchan in Val d' Europe. Or just bring snacks from home.

4. **Take your own photos** - If you do not want to pay €15 for a character photo, take one yourself - the Cast Members will not mind. They will even take the photo for you, if you ask them.

5. **Combine photos** - If you are going on multiple attractions, paying €15 for a single on-ride photo can start to eat into your budget when visiting multiple rides. The same thing applies to official character photos. See our section on Photopass for a great way to save money.

6. **Take your own costumes/plushes** - If your little boy or girl wants to buy a dress or outfit in the Disney parks, there is a way that you can save money – purchasing these items outside of Disneyland Paris is substantially cheaper from other Disney stores, online or at supermarkets. Just buy them before you leave for Disneyland Paris and pack them secretly. Give your child the costume once you arrive and they will be over the moon. The same applies to Disney soft toys, or toys bought at home.

7. **Try more affordable meals** - Although food prices are expensive there are some better value restaurants than others – these of course will depend on your tastes. Also, try the meal deals where you can get a main course, dessert and drink for one price. Alternatively try a buffet as a late lunch, and then just have a snack for dinner.

8. **Use Fastpass** – It will save you hours in queuing time (see Chapter 9: Fastpass for more information on this free time saving service).

Chapter 16
# Dining
## Introduction:
There are a huge variety of places to eat at Disneyland Paris. Food options vary from sandwich and snack locations, to fast food, character buffets, table-service dining and even high-class dining. This section goes the different types of restaurant, meal plans available and other important food-related information.

There are several different types of restaurant at the resort:
**Buffet Restaurants** – These are all you can eat locations where you fill up your plate from all the food offered as many times as you want throughout the meal – you can stay as long as you want to. Buffet meals may or may not include drinks, depending on the location.
**Counter Service/Quick Service** – This works just like any other big high street fast food chain – you look at the menus above the cashiers, you pay for your food and you collect it a few minutes later. You will find everything from burgers and chips, to chicken, to pizza and pasta. However, do be aware that Disney 'fast'-food locations are notoriously slow and a queue of just four or five people in front of you can easily mean a wait time of twenty to thirty minutes.
**Sit Down/Table Service** – These are restaurants where you order from a menu, are served by a waiter who then brings your food to your table.
**Character Buffets** – These are available throughout the day and are all-you-can eat places where characters come around to interact with you and take photos.

**Top Tip**: Whether it be a snack cart, a quick service location or a full service location – you are never obliged to order from the set menu. Ordering specific items 'a la carte' is completely fine, although it may save you money if you order certain menu combinations.

**Additional notes:**
- For buffets, kids' prices apply for those aged 3 to 11.
- When staying at a Disney hotel you have a breakfast buffet included every morning of your stay. You may have the option of having breakfast in the parks or in the Disney Village for an extra fee. Ask at reception for availability.
- Adults can generally order from the kids' menu, especially at counter service locations.
- For an idea of how much food is likely to cost, check out the parks chapters which give you the prices of menus and a la carte main courses, as well as some individual items.
- Not all restaurants may have a vegan or vegetarian option but Cast Members and the chefs will do their best to accommodate you. If you can call in advance to alert them and make a reservation, this will help you greatly.

## Meal Plans:

Meal Plans are an option offered to guests who book packages with a hotel and park tickets together – the meal plans allow you to pre-purchase meal vouchers at the time of booking, meaning that when you arrive at the parks you will not need to worry about the cost of meals. The meal plans work on a paper voucher system which are given to guests when they check-in to their hotel.

To use the vouchers, simply hand them over when it is time to pay. Make sure to look out for which restaurants accept which meal plans. If you wish to go to a restaurant that is not included on your specific meal plan, these can be used at the face value amount that is printed on the vouchers. E.g. If you have 'Plus' voucher but want to visit a 'Premium' restaurant you can do this and the 'Plus' voucher value will be deducted from your bill. You will pay the difference.

A meal voucher includes a set menu or buffet, plus one soft drink. There are three different meal plans from you to choose from, these vary in price - the more expensive meal plans include the most expensive restaurants and items.

| Restaurant Name | Restaurant type | Location | Included in Standard Plan? | Included in Plus Plan? | Included in Premium Plan? |
|---|---|---|---|---|---|
| Agrabah Cafe | Buffet | Disneyland Park | Yes | Yes | Yes |
| Annette's Diner | Table Service | Disney Village | Yes | Yes | Yes |
| Auberge de Cendrillon | Table Service | Disneyland Park | No | No | Yes |
| Beaver Creek Tavern | Table Service | Sequoia Lodge Hotel | No | Yes | Yes |
| Blue Lagoon | Table Service | Disneyland Park | No | Yes | Yes |
| Buffalo Bill's Wild West Show | Table Service Show | Disney Village | No | No | Yes |
| Cafe Mickey | Table Service Character Dining | Disney Village | No | Yes | Yes |
| California Grill | Table Service | Disneyland Hotel | No | No | Yes |
| Cape Cod | Buffet | Newport Bay Club Hotel | No | Yes | Yes |
| Chuck Wagon Cafe | Buffet | Disney Village | Yes | Yes | Yes |
| Crockett's Tavern | Buffet | Davy Crockett's Ranch Campsite | Yes | Yes | Yes |
| Hunter's Grill | Buffet | Sequoia Lodge Hotel | No | Yes | Yes |
| Inventions | Buffet Character Dining | Disneyland Hotel | No | No | Yes |
| La Cantina | Buffet | Sante Fe Hotel | Yes | Yes | Yes |
| La Grange at Billy Bob's | Table Service | Disney Village | Yes | Yes | Yes |
| Manhattan Restaurant | Table Service | Hotel New York | No | Yes | Yes |
| Plaza Gardens | Buffet | Disneyland Park | Yes | Yes | Yes |
| Parkside Diner | Buffet | Hotel New York | No | Yes | Yes |
| Restaurant des Stars | Buffet | Walt Disney Studios Park | Yes | Yes | Yes |
| Silver Spur Steakhouse | Table Service | Disneyland Park | Yes | Yes | Yes |
| The Steakhouse | Table Service | Disney Village | No | Yes | Yes |
| Walt's: An American Restaurant | Table Service | Disneyland Park | No | Yes | Yes |
| Yacht Club | Table Service | Newport Bay Club Hotel | No | Yes | Yes |

The vouchers can also be used at most Counter/Quick Service dining locations but we do not recommend doing this as the vouchers are often worth more than the meals and therefore they would be going to waste.

Meal plans when used wisely can save you up to 15% off the full price, but circumstances will vary from person to person. For many people, simply having the piece of mind of having pre-paid meals is worth the price.

When booking you can either choose a half-board option for one pre-paid meal per day or a full-board option for two pre-paid meals per day.

For arrivals until 1$^{st}$ April 2015, prices are as follows. For arrivals from 1$^{st}$ April 2015 until 23$^{rd}$ March 2016 prices will be between £1 and £3 more per person per night.

|  | Standard Adult | Standard Child | Plus Adult | Plus Child | Premium Adult | Premium Child |
|---|---|---|---|---|---|---|
| Full board | £39/€46 | £19/€23 | £49/€59 | £23/€28 | £83/€99 | £41/€49 |
| Half board | £22/€26 | £11/€13 | £28/€33 | £13/€15 | £48/€57 | £24/€29 |

As well as your two standard meals per day, guests purchasing the Standard, Plus or Premium Meal Plans will also be offered a "Pause Gourmande" (teatime treat consisting of one cold or hot drink plus a sweet treat).

Table service meals are from a set menu on the "Standard" and "Plus" plans. Those on the premium plan will still be able to order a la carte from table service restaurants. If in doubt simply asking your waiter before ordering and show them the vouchers you have.

**Top Tip**: If you stay at Disney's Davy Crockett Ranch and book a Meal Plan, breakfast is included. (It is already included in all other Disney hotels without the need for a meal plan).

There is also a "Hotel Meal Plan" offered where price varies by hotel:

|  | Santa Fe, Cheyenne and Davy Crockett's Ranch "Hotel Meal Plan" Adult | Santa Fe, Cheyenne and Davy Crockett's Ranch "Hotel Meal Plan" Child | Sequoia Lodge, Newport Bay Club and Hotel New York "Hotel Meal Plan" Adult | Sequoia Lodge, Newport Bay Club and Hotel New York "Hotel Meal Plan" Child | Disneyland Hotel "Hotel Meal Plan" Adult | Disneyland Hotel "Hotel Meal Plan" Child |
|---|---|---|---|---|---|---|
| Full board | £29/€35 | £16/€19 | £35/€42 | £18/€21 | £64/€77 | £35/€42 |
| Half board | £19/€23 | £11/€13 | £25/€30 | £13/€15 | £45/€53 | £23/€28 |

The half board plan includes one dinner buffet voucher at a restaurant at your hotel. The full board plan includes one dinner buffet voucher at a restaurant at your hotel plus a lunch voucher for a menu at one counter service location in the Disney parks.

## Making Reservations:

If you want to guarantee you will be able to dine at a specific restaurant, it is worth booking advance. You can book your restaurant up to 60 days in advance, but in reality booking even two weeks or less beforehand will usually get you a table. Most people do not book restaurants in theme parks in Europe in advance, which is a stark change from the American Disney parks. Despite this, it is worth making a reservation as early as possible just in case you want a specific meal on a specific day. Plus, you will be seated much faster with a reservation that without one.

You can call the Dining Reservation hotline in advance on +33 (0)1 60 30 40 50 and can book in several languages, including English. You can also book at City Hall in Disneyland Park, Studio Services in Walt Disney Studios or at any of the Disney hotel lobbies.

You do not need to be staying in a Disney hotel to book a table at a restaurant. If you cannot attend a reservation, it is good practice to cancel it.

In low season we have often walked up to restaurants on the day and got reservations for the same day or the next day. In the high season this becomes significantly more difficult.

## Tipping in Restaurants:

In France, a 15% service charge is required by law to be included in your menu prices. Although this may not be itemised in the bill it is *always* included – you are not expected to leave any additional money as service has been paid for in the bill. If you particularly liked the service you are of course free to leave a few euros as a tip, €4 to €8 would be the maximum really for an €80 meal.

Sometimes in France, waiters will not return with your change and assume it is their tip - if this was not your intention, make this known. One easy way to avoid this is to always pay by credit or debit card. This website has more information on tipping in restaurants and other establishments - http://www.tiny.cc/tippinginfrance.

Chapter 17
# Useful to know
## When to visit:
Crowds in Disneyland Paris vary greatly from season to season and even from day to day, the difference of a single day can save you hundreds of euros in accommodation costs, as well as hours of queuing. You will have to consider the national holidays in France and all surrounding countries, the weather, school holidays, pricing and more to find the best time for your visit. To help you with that we have compiled a detailed guide of when we think the best times to go to Disneyland Paris are, even including a detailed analysis of weekdays.

Below is a guide to the best times of the year to visit Disneyland Paris and the times of the year to avoid.

**Major French/European Holidays - in calendar order: (times to avoid if possible)**
- 1st January - New Year's Day
- 1st January to 4th January - School Christmas holidays
- Around 15th February to 1st March - French school break, and half-term in the UK
- 17th March - St. Patrick's Day (extra Disney celebrations including fireworks means larger crowds)
- April to Early May - Depending on when Easter Falls. Two weeks before and after Easter Sunday
- 1st May - Labour Day / May Day
- 8th May - Bank holiday - Victory in Europe Day
- Varies - Ascension Day - The sixth Thursday after Easter
- Varies - Pentecost - 10 days after Ascension Day
- Varies - Whit Monday - 2nd Monday after Ascension Day/Day after Pentecost.
- 15th June to 15th September - Combination of European School Summer Holidays
- 14th July - Bastille Day (Bank holiday)

- 15th August – Assumption of Mary
- Middle of October - Start of November - French/UK Half-Term and Halloween
- 15th December - 31st December - Christmas Holidays. 31st December is particularly busy.

The day of the week which you visit can also make a large difference to crowd sizes and your ride waiting times - a ride can have an average wait time of 90 minutes on one day and just 30 minutes the next.

Wednesdays are particularly nasty, as schools in France do not have lessons on Wednesdays. This means higher than expected crowd numbers as kids, particularly teenagers, go for a mid-week trip to Disney. Weekends too are to be avoided even during less busy seasons.

Below is a rating of the **best days of the week** to visit - from best to worst:

The best day of the week to visit is Monday, followed by Tuesday, then Thursday, then Wednesday, Friday, Sunday, and finally the busiest day of the week is by far Saturday.

The exception to this is during the Summer school holidays where Wednesday is actually one of the better days to attend but Saturday and Sunday will still be particularly busy, next worse are Monday and Tuesday due to families taking extended weekend breaks, usually starting on Saturday and finishing on a Tuesday.

Therefore the **best times of the year** to visit are usually cheaper and out of season (meaning you will probably need to ask the school for permission to take your kids). They are:
- Early December to Mid-December – Going during this time of the year also means you will get to see all the Christmas decorations and entertainment. Make sure to visit before schools are on holiday. The weather will be cold.

- January - Excluding the first four or five days, when it is still school holidays, in general this is a good time to visit. The weather will be very cold.
- First half of February – The weather will be very cold, but equally with low crowd numbers.
- Second half of March to about two weeks before Easter (April) – There will be low crowds, but the weather will still be relatively cold.
- April - Excluding the two weeks before and after Easter Sunday.
- May - Excluding the aforementioned bank holidays. At this time of the year the weather is improving but it is certainly not T-shirt and shorts weather.
- The first two weeks of June – Starting to get warmer, and with low crowds before the school holidays.
- After mid-September to the first half of October – The kids are back at school and the weather is quite nice. This is perhaps the best time of year to go. Plus, in October you can see the Halloween decorations and entertainment
- The second week of November until mid-December – The weather is getting colder but there are low crowds. Going during this time of the year also means you will get to see all the Christmas decorations and entertainment.

## Mobile phone apps:

Disneyland Paris has its own free iOS (iPhone, iPad and iPod) and Android apps, which allow you to enhance your trip before and during your visit. With the apps you can plan your sty including an overview of the hotels on offer, and a look at the different attractions throughout the resort. You can even create an itinerary. When you are at the resort itself you can check out the opening hours of the parks, timings of shows and parades, and you can even see the attraction wait times. It is this last feature that makes the app the most useful – no more checking out the Tip board at the end of Main street for all the wait times, you can just check them in the palm of your hand, and for both parks at the same time. Be aware that you will need a data connection to make use of this application which means you must have data roaming enabled on your phone. Data usage is minimal for the app. Unlike Walt Disney World, at Disneyland Paris there is no free Wi-Fi though this is a project that the resort is currently working on.

## On-ride photos:

Capture that magical moment!
Many of Disneyland Paris' rides have specially placed cameras which are positioned and timed to take perfect on-ride photos of you and your family at the most action filled moments on the parks' attractions. Buy the photo and you will have a photo of you at the fastest, steepest, scariest and most fun point of the ride. The result? Some timeless memories.

When you get off the ride you will go past some monitors which show you a preview of your photo (usually with some sort of watermark on top). If you wish to purchase it, simply go to the photo counter. You do not have to buy on-ride photos straight after your ride either. In fact, you can pick them up at any time during the day. Just remember your unique number at the ride exit or ask a member of staff at the photo kiosk to write it down for you.

If you like the photo, Cast Members will show it to you up close before you have to pay for it. If you like it - buy it! It's really one of those memories you will always remember.

Photo print prices are €15 for one photo, €20 for two photos and €25 for three photos.

The attractions with on-ride photos are: Big Thunder Mountain, Pirates of the Caribbean, Space Mountain: Mission 2, Buzz Lightyear Laser Blast, Rock n' Rollercoaster, and The Twilight Zone: Tower of Terror.

**Top Tip**: If you want photos from different rides you can combine these together on a Photopass. See our section on Photopass below to find out how to save a lot of money on photos by not purchasing them individually.

## Photopass:

Disneyland Paris' Photopass is an easy to use system that makes collecting all your in-park photos as easy as can be. Simply go up to any in-park photographer (including those stationed at Meet Mickey Mouse and Princess Pavilion, and other characters) and have your photo taken, and ask for a Disney Photopass. Alternatively you can ask for this card at any ride photo counter (this option is often not advertised but is available if you ask). This same card can then be re-used throughout both parks anywhere you find a photographer or with on-ride photos – simply hand over your card and any photos throughout your visit will be added onto it and all kept together on the system. Photos are saved on the Photopass system for 7 days each. For annual Passholders, photos can be saved onto your annual pass for 90 days.

Before your photos expire make sure to visit one of these locations to view and purchase your photos: New Century Notions: Flora's Unique Boutique in Disneyland Park, Walt Disney Studios Store in Walt Disney Studios Park, and The Disney Gallery in Disney Village. Photos can also be viewed at the shops inside any of the onsite hotels. At these locations you can them purchase prints and/or digital versions.

If you amass multiple Photopass cards, they can be combined into one when purchasing your photos too.

Pricing is as follows: €16 for 1 photo, €21 for 2 photos, €26 for 3 photos, €31 for 4 photos, subsequent photos cost €5 each. At an individual rate the photos may seem expensive but when you purchase more the prices start to seem very reasonable indeed.

Add an extra element of Disney magic with themed borders and details, which can be added to your photos at no additional cost.

For those who have used the Photopass system in the US parks, the Disneyland Paris system works in a similar manner but the prints are generally more reasonably priced here. There are also digital mobile options available in France which are not available in the US. The biggest difference, however, is the lack of Photopass photographers throughout the parks in France whereas there are several of them in each park in the US, allowing you to get great photos with the parks' icons. We expect this to arrive in Paris in the near future.

## Photopass+

Photopass+ is the revolutionary new system that makes finding, collecting and choosing your in-park photographs even easier. Photos with characters and ride photos are now part of one easy to use system. The system was launched in late 2014.

Photopass+ is priced at €49,99 for unlimited digital photos of your Disneyland Paris trip. When Photopass+ is purchased guests will get a Photopass+ card and lanyard to make it easy to add photos onto the account.

In addition, two mini cards will also be included so that each family member can have their own card and easily add photos from their visit to the same account – this allows, for example, a mum to ride Big Thunder Mountain with the kids and add on-ride photos to the account at the same time that Dad rides Space Mountain: Mission 2 and add his on-ride photo to the same account. Guests can add an unlimited number of photos to their account for up to 10 days following their Photopass+ activation.

Guests are able to create an online account at www.disneyphotopass.eu or via the iOS and Android 'Disneyland Paris Photopass' mobile apps. If you are using the mobile app, you can simply scan the QR code on the ride photo preview monitors and have it added to your account without the need to visit the ride photo counters. Alternatively, guests can type in the photo number as it appears on these photo preview screens.

Guests can view their photos on the DisneyPhotopass.eu website and download them in high quality, as well as buy prints, photo books, calendars, gifts and more. Photos will remain on the website until one year after they were taken, at which point they will become unavailable – this gives you plenty of time to download your photos.

The Photopass+ system that is being launched at Disneyland Paris is very similar to the system that is already in use in the US parks – but this one is more reasonably priced, especially for prints of your photos. One feature which is unique to the Disneyland Paris resort at the moment is incorporated into the mobile applications. Guests are able to purchase a single digital version of their on-ride photo for £2.99/€3,59 each, or six on-ride photos for £7.99/€9,99.

Guests who pre-book Photopass+ as part of their stay will get a €10 discount. Guests who have pre-booked Photopass+ will be given a voucher at check-in which must then be exchanged for the actual product at the theme parks' store. Annual pass discounts are also available when buying in the park – as of may 2015, annual passholders will get a Photopass+ valid for one year from the date of purchase, offering fantastic value for money.

## Baby Switch and Rider Switch:

The Baby Switch system is a valuable timesaving solution that allows parents to reduce queuing time throughout their visit whilst experiencing thrill attractions.

One common issue at a theme park is when two adults want to do a rollercoaster but they have a child who is not tall enough to ride – they can either take it in turns and do the ride (queuing twice) or they can not experience the attraction at all. Disney's Baby Switch service allows one adult to queue up and ride whilst the other stays with the child, then the second adult will be able to ride as soon as the first one returns to take care of the child – but the second adult will be granted almost immediate access to the ride, usually through the exit, bypassing the entire queue line. Each adult will experience the ride separately but the second adult will not need to wait in line.

The system varies from attraction to attraction so make sure to ask a Cast Member at the entrance how the system works with that particular ride.

This system used to be known as Baby Switch but it has officially been renamed Rider Switch to accommodate all kinds of ages – this means you do not necessarily have to have a child or baby present to use this service. Whether you call it Baby Switch, or Rider Switch, the principles are the same.

## Parking:

Many guests choose to visit Disneyland Paris by car, as it is the most practical and/or affordable way for them to travel. If you will be doing this, simply follow the signs to theme park parking when you are nearby. Parking is charged for all guests except some Annual Passholders and Disney hotel guests. The price is €15 per car, €20 for a caravan and €10 for a motorbike.

From the parking area to the theme parks is a ten to fifteen minute walk including walking on several travelators. This depends on where exactly you have parked within the car park.

Guests staying at on-site Disney hotels get a free shuttle service to the park, but can also opt to drive to the theme parks instead – these guests get complimentary parking at the theme park parking lot included in the price of their room and can park for no additional cost. To be honest, it is rare to save any time by taking your own car instead of the hotel shuttles, which only take a few minutes to reach the theme parks from the hotels.

**Top Tip:** Instead of parking at the main Disneyland Paris theme park car park, follow signs to Disney Village. Disney Village has its very own multi-story Vinci car park which is located just a two minute walk from the theme parks – significantly closer than the official parking location. The price is also more favourable at €12 for a day, instead of €15. Additionally, there are usually no queues for the Disney Village Vinci car park before park opening and after park closing. The same can definitely not be said for the Disneyland Paris theme park car parking area where leaving the area can take a while in the evening.

## Single Rider Queue Lines:
One of the best ways to significantly reduce your time waiting in queue lines is to use the Single Rider line instead of the regular queue line. This is available at selected attractions across the resort.

A Single Rider Line is a completely separate queue line that is used to fill free spaces on ride vehicles. For example, if a ride vehicle can seat 8 people and a group of 4 turns up, and then a group of 3 is placed in the same vehicle, then a single rider will be put onto the ride from the Single Rider Line – this fills up the empty space on the ride vehicle whilst also allowing guests who are willing to ride with strangers to wait for significantly less time.

When the theme parks get extremely busy, it is possible that single rider lines be temporarily closed - this happens when the wait in the single rider line is the same or greater than the regular line thereby undermining its purpose. Conversely, if the theme parks are not very busy, then sometimes Single Rider Lines may not operate as they will not provide any time savings.

Single Rider Lines can be used for a group of riders too, its not just for individuals - just be aware that members of the group will not ride with each other and you will each be in a different vehicle. You can, of course, just meet each other at the exit of the ride.

Selected attractions operate Single Rider Lines. The following attractions have this system in operation:
- RC Racer
- Toy Soldier Parachute Drop
- Crush's Coaster
- Ratatouille: The Adventure – This is by far the Single Rider Line which saves you the most amount of time.

Disneyland Paris has announced that it wishes to add one new single rider line per year to new or existing attractions over the new few years so you can expect the selection to increase in the future.

## Extra Magic Hours:

Extra Magic Hours (EMH) allow selected guests up to two hours of extra theme park access at Disneyland Paris each morning – this allows these guests to get access to an almost empty theme park and selected attractions with little to no wait. There will also be the opportunity to meet Disney characters before other guests get to the park, which will significantly reduce your wait.

Most commonly Extra Magic Hours operate at Disneyland Park for two hours each morning – this happens during over 90% of the year. At selected times of the year this is reduced to one hour or one hour and a half when the theme parks open earlier. Additionally, Extra Magic Hours have been offered at Walt Disney Studios Park for two hours on selected dates too for the past few years. At very peak periods in 2014 such as the two weeks around Christmas, EMHs were offered at both parks daily. It is unclear whether this will return in the future.

## How can I get Extra Magic Hours?
The Extra Magic Hours benefit is available exclusively to guests staying at on-site Disney Hotels – but not selected or partner hotels. Extra Magic Hours are also available for guests who have the Dream Annual Passport and Fantasy Annual Passport.

Disney hotel guests will need their park tickets and their Easy Pass (given at check-in) to be allowed entry during Extra Magic Hours.

## Is the whole park open during EMH?
Unfortunately not the whole park is open during Extra Magic Hours – at Disneyland Park selected attractions in Fantasyland and Discoveryland operate, as well as Main Street USA.

Disneyland Paris does not publish a list of the rides which are operational during this period. Typically the following rides are available during EMH – other rides and lands will open with the opening of the park to all guests:
**Fantasyland** – Dumbo: The Flying Elephant, Peter Pan's Flight, The Adventures of Pinocchio, Lancelot's Carrousel and Mad Hatter's Teacups.
**Discoveryland** - Space Mountain, Buzz Lightyear Laser Blast and Orbitron.

Extra Magic Hours at Walt Disney Studios are still a relatively new addition – as such there is no guarantee of what attractions will be offered. In the past the following attractions have been offered: *The Twilight Zone: Tower of Terror, Rock n' Rollercoaster, Crush's Coaster, Cars: Quatre Roues Rallye, Ratatouille: The Adventure, Toy Soldiers Parachute Drop, Slinky Dog Zigzag Spin and RC Racer*. In our opinion, the Extra Magic Hours at the Studio's are hugely valuable and offer more time savings than at Disneyland Park overall, especially for thrill seekers.

## Any more details?

Extra Magic Hours start at 8:00am meaning that two lands of Disneyland Park are open from that time until the official park opening (which is usually 10:00am(. This benefit is available exclusively to Disney Hotel guests, and Dream and Fantasy Annual Passholders only. Extra Magic Hours are usually offered daily but may be reduced during quieter periods of the year. Make sure to consult our website at www.independentguidebooks.com/dlp/hours for park hours including Extra Magic hours (listed as EMH).

Extra Magic Hours can be reduced in length or even change to the Walt Disney Studios Park as have previously been mentioned in this section.

# Assorted Questions & Answers:
### How much French do I need to know?

All Cast Members at the resort speak French. Most Cast Members at the resort speak English, so for the most part the language barrier is not a problem when talking to the parks' employees. However, knowing the basics in French is really helpful, and people do appreciate it if you say "Bonjour" and "Merci" and then switch to English, or even better say "Parlez-vous Anglais?" [pronounced *par-lay-voo-zarn-glay*] for "Do you speak English?".

Additionally, you may occasionally come across a Cast Member with a limited grasp of the English language, which can make things more difficult. Cast Members do speak many other languages too – with Spanish and Italian being some of the most commonly spoken ones.

## Do I need to carry my purchases around with me all day?

If you have bought a toy, t-shirt, ornament or anything else from a Disney shop you do not have to carry it with you all day. When paying for your goods before 3:00pm simply ask to use the Disney Shopping Service – this allows you to leave your items at the store, go and enjoy the parks and then pick up your purchases later in the day.

You can then either pick up your purchases at the World of Disney store at Disney Village in the evening, or at the Disney boutiques at on-site Disney hotels and selected partner hotels.

## What currency is used in France?

France uses Euros as its currency. If you come from a country that does not use euros as its currency them you can either exchange cash before you go, or use a debit card or credit card to pay for your purchases whilst in France – be aware that most banks add additional fees when paying by card in a foreign country and/or currency.

Traveller's cheques are accepted at Disneyland Paris but we do not recommend these. We recommend using a Pre-paid debit card from a company such as FairFX (for UK readers only but other similar companies are available in other countries). These pre-paid cards allow you to top-up the card with as many Euros as you would like, like a mobile phone top up works. The card is then delivered in mail to you. You can then use the card for purchases with no additional fees when abroad.

If you do plan on using FairFx there is usually a £9.95 account opening fee – however if you use this link - http://bit.ly/debitdlp - then there are no fees associated with purchasing the card. If you deposit over £250 in your first transaction you will also get an additional £2.50 an extra to spend for free.

For guests who prefer to change money at the theme parks there are Bureau des Changes located at both theme parks and in the Disney Village. These operate limited opening hours – in addition the rates offered are not usually very good, but it is another option.

## Is there a time difference?
France uses the UTC+1 time zone, which is used throughout most of Central and Western Europe. The UK and Portugal operate on UTC time and therefore 1:00pm in the UK is 2:00pm in France. Some countries in Eastern Europe such as Ukraine and Latvia use the UTC+2 time zone so 3:00pm in Latvia is 2:00pm in France.

We recommend that you set your watches, alarm clocks and mobile phone clocks to French time as soon as you board your flight, train or ferry to France – or as soon as you cross the French border for those travelling by car. By doing this you will make sure that you are in the correct time zone for things such as check-in times, opening hours and Fastpass return times. It is also vital to make sure you do not miss your return flights or trains on the way back home.

## Can I re-enter a theme park after I leave it on the same day?
Of course you can. Simply ask a Cast Member to stamp your hand on the way out of the park. Then, the same day when at the turnstiles to enter the park, scan your hand under the ultraviolet light and put your ticket in to the turnstile.

The hand stamp system is sometimes not in operation. If this is the case, you will merely need your park ticket for re-entry – be sure to get a stamp anyway to be sure.

## Can I take food into the parks?
Even though there are checkpoints and bag searches on the way in, these are there for safety reasons and are looking for anything that may harm you and other visitors. These security checkpoints are not there to prevent you from taking food into the parks.

You can take snacks, sandwiches and drinks into the parks, as well as baby milk, which restaurants will happily heat for you. Picnics are forbidden so do not expect to lay down a blanket and have a meal on the grass in the theme parks. Find a bench instead – we particularly like the area near the Frontierland Disneyland Railroad station due to the large amount of seating available. Additionally, there is a picnic area located outside the theme parks – simply ask a Cast Member at the exit of the parks.

Glass containers are not allowed in the parks, including glass bottles.

## Are there any baby facilities?
Each park has its own Baby Care Centre with microwaves, bottle warmers, high chairs, changing tables. These locations are designed to be comfortable and quiet, and can be a good escape from the parks when these are busy. Nappies and baby food are also available for sale at selected locations.

## What I fall ill or get injured?
Disneyland Paris makes safety its number one priority and everything is done to ensure you have a safe visit. Unfortunately, it is possible that some guests fall ill or become injured whilst at the resort – each park has a First Aid Centre with qualified staff to help you with any problems. If more serious intervention is required Disneyland Paris has its own licensed emergency services department, and also works very closely with outside hospitals and agencies.

## Is there a prayer room?
Although there is not a dedicated prayer room, Disneyland Paris does make accommodations for this. If you require a prayer room within the theme parks please visit City Hall or Studio Services where they can arrange for a room for you to use for this purpose.

## Are there lockers for me to store my belongings?
When Disneyland Paris originally opened in 1992 there were lockers located inside Disneyland Park. However, security has tightened up over recent years and there are now no self-storage luggage services inside the theme parks themselves. Instead, there are two luggage services located just outside the theme park entrances where you hand your bag to a Cast Member and they put it in storage behind the counter.

At Disneyland Park 'Luggage Services' is located to the right of the main entrance by the Guest Relations window. At Walt Disney Studios Park, luggage storage is located to the right of the ticket windows. There is also an automatic left luggage storage facility available inside Marne-La-Vallee – Chessy rail station on the upper level – Disneyland Paris does not operate this service in the train station.

Lockers at the parks and in the station range in price from €5 to €10 depending on the size of locker and number of bags needed to be stored. For the station lockers you need change (there is a change machine inside the luggage room) whereas at the Disney parks you can get change from the person serving you and pay by card too. If you are a Dream Annual Passport holder you may store one item in left luggage per day at the theme parks at no cost.

You can access the Disneyland Paris lockers at the parks as many times as you want throughout a day to get food or other items without being charged more than once. With the station lockers every time you open the lockers, you must pay again to lock them.

## What are some useful French phrases?
Hello/Good morning - *Bonjour*

Good evening - *Bonsoir*
Do you speak English? - *Parlez-vous anglais?*
How much does this cost? - *Combien ça coûte?*
Thanks - *Merci!*
No problem - *De rien*
Can you take a photo of us please? - *Pouvez-vous nous prendre une photo s'il vous plaît?*
Yes - *Oui*
No - *Non*
A little / a bit - *Un peu*
Rare (for meat) – *Saignante*
Medium-Rare (for meat) – *A pointe*
Well-done/well-cooked (for meat) – *Bien Cuite*
Very well-cooked (for meat) – *Tres Bien Cuite*

## How can I celebrate a birthday?

There are several ways to celebrate a birthday at Disneyland Paris. If you are dining at any table service restaurant you can add a cake to your meal for €27. We recommend making a restaurant reservation by calling the dining booking line and mentioning the cake in advance.

Additionally, guests can visit City Hall and Studio Services to be given a 'Happy Birthday' sticker to wear throughout the day. To keep the younger guests happy, make sure to ask the Cast Members at City Hall whether any of the characters have a special message for your child – you will be lead into a room, and then the phone will ring. When your child picks the phone up there will be a recorded message wishing them a happy birthday – this can make for some incredible memories.

## Are there any local religious restrictions?

According to the gov.uk travel advice website "Concealing the face in public places in France is illegal. This includes balaclavas, full veils or any other garment or mask that is used to conceal the face. Failure to comply with the ban is punishable by a maximum fine of €150. Under this law, forcing someone to hide their face is also a crime and is punishable by a year's imprisonment and a fine of up to €30,000. If the person forced to hide their face is a minor, the sentence is doubled. The law does not provide any exemption for tourists." This is not a choice Disney has made, but the government's – at Disneyland Paris, however, you will find people covering their face for religious reasons; they will not be fined when on private property such as Disneyland Paris.

## Renting Wheelchairs and Buggies/Strollers/Pushchairs

Wheelchair and pushchair rentals are available at Disneyland Paris for those who do not wish to bring their own with them. You are of course welcome to bring your own pushchair or wheelchair with you if you wish.

If your child is recently out of a pushchair it may still be worth hiring one as it is likely your kids will get tired due to the huge walking distances involved with a Disneyland Paris visit. Sometimes it is nice to just let them sit in their pushchair and have a break. It should be noted that Disneyland Paris' pushchairs do not recline, and do not have any sort of rain protection. We have also had reports from some guests that say that the pushchairs are not the most comfortable.

The daily cost for hiring a wheelchair or pushchair is €15. The deposit required for a wheelchair is €150; this is €70 for a pushchair if you wish to be able to take these out of the parks, move between parks or enter the Disney Village.

Chapter 18

# How to spend less time queuing

Disneyland Paris meticulously themes its queue lines to immerse you into the atmosphere and to begin to tell the story of the ride you about to get on, but sometimes you just want to forget queuing and get on the rides as quickly as possible.

It is important to remember that a visit to a theme park will inevitably involve waiting in queue lines. However, if you do not set out with a strategy then you will spend much longer in queues than you need to. This chapter covers our top tips on minimising your wait times:

- **Eat outside the usual normal hours** – This is difficult for some people to imagine but you will have to queue to order your food. Whether you want a meal at a table service restaurant or a counter service meal, waiting is part of the game. If you can have lunch before midday or after 3:00pm you will experience much shorter waits. In addition having dinner before 8:00pm will also guarantee you a shorter wait in line.
- **Counter service meal tricks** - Many guests are especially caught by surprise of waits of 45 minutes or more at counter service restaurants, especially at peak times – remember to eat outside the usual meal times as our aforementioned tip explains. In addition, at quick service locations each cashier will have two lines and alternate from one line to the next – try and calculate how many groups (families), and not people, are in front of you in the line. There may be ten people in front of you in one queue line but only two families, whereas the other queue line may have just five people but from five different families. The line with ten people will move more quickly as there are only two orders to process as opposed to the other line.
- **Disney hotel guests** - If you are staying at a Disney hotel take advantage of Extra Magic Hours - you get entry into one of the theme parks up to two whole hours before regular guests do. During

this time you can experience many (but not all) of the parks' attractions with minimal waits. See our Extra Magic Hours section for more details.

- **Disneyland Park opens early** - Disneyland Park's opening hours usually state it officially opens at 10:00am, but any guest the park 30 minutes earlier from 9.30am - this means you can enter the park, enjoy the atmosphere, eat breakfast, start shopping and take photos of Main street USA and Sleeping Beauty Castle. At the end of Main Street USA when you arrive to the hub in front of the castle, the entrances to all the lands will be cordoned off by Cast Members. If you are a Disney hotel guest or a Fantasy or Dream annual pass holder show your EasyPass and you can enter Fantasyland and Discoveryland. Otherwise wait by the ropes at the entrances of the lands for "rope-drop" when it is announced that the park is now open. You will be reminded to "walk to your first destination" please. If you are there before the official park opening time, you can be on your first ride within minutes.

- **Walt Disney Studios opens early** - At Walt Disney Studios Park, the park also opens at 9:30am. At that time you can walk around the entire park and queue outside attraction entrances. Most attractions will not start operating until 10:00am and the park's official opening but some may do so.

- **Crush's coaster does NOT have a Fastpass queue** - If you plan on experiencing Crush's Coaster, we cannot overstate how important it is for you to be at Walt Disney Studios Park's turnstiles before 9:30am. By doing this you will be able to go through the turnstiles as soon as the park pre-opens and start making your way to Crush's Coaster. This attraction usually starts operating slightly before the park officially opens. See Chapter 11: Touring Plans for more details on how to maximize your time at the park. Alternatively, use the single rider queue throughout the day which can save you time too.

- **Ignore the parades and fireworks** - If you have already seen the parades, shows or fireworks, use that time to ride attractions as the queues are often much shorter. If you have not seen these before, we do not recommend you skip them to ride an attraction; attractions are generally open all day, whereas these parades and shows are often only performed at select times of the day and are attractions themselves – plus these are what separate the Disney theme parks

from the competition!
- **Ride outdoor attractions during the rain** – Outdoor attractions such as Dumbo, Flying Carpets over Agrabah, Casey Junior, Storybook Canal boats, Big Thunder Mountain, Indiana Jones et le Temple du Peril, Slinky Dog Zigzag Spin, Toy Soldiers Parachute Drop and RC Racer have significantly reduced queues when it is raining. Yes, you may get soaked whilst riding (although a poncho will prevent this) but you will also wait for a significantly lower amount of time in the queue line. **Author's Note**: One of my favourite Disneyland Paris memories is riding Dumbo, Snow White and the Seven Dwarves, and Lancelot's Carrousel, followed by Flying Carpets over Agrabah in the pouring rain on my birthday. Yes, I was soaked but it is I will always remember and made for unforgettable photos. **Top Tip**: You will find that many guests will return to hotel if it begins raining so even some of the indoor rides will have shorter queues when there is inclement weather.
- **See our section on the less busy times** - If you are visiting on New Year's Day expect to queue a lot longer than in the middle of September. If you are going on a weekend expect to wait more than on a weekday. See our section entitled When to visit and make the most of your time at the parks.
- **Go shopping at the start or end of the day** - If you enter the park during the pre-opening period from 9:30am to 10:00am, this is a perfect time to go shopping. Alternatively, go shopping at the end of the day - even when the park is "officially" closed, the shops on Main Street USA stay open about an hour longer than the rest of the park. Alternatively, just walk over to Disney Village in the evening and go shopping there up until 1:00am on most days! Additionally, all the on-site hotels as well as selected partner hotels have a small Disney boutique inside them. Do not waste your time during the day shopping, do it at strategic times and make the most of your visit.
- **Pick up your Times Guide on the way in** - Get your Park Map and the Times Guide on the way in – you will usually find them being distributed together. The Times Guide lists all time sensitive information at the parks – it means that you will know the timings of parades, shows, character appearances and more. As such, you are sure not to waste time going back and forth to find out that a character you saw earlier on the day, has now left that location.

Chapter 19
# Disneyland Paris for Walt Disney World Regulars

Many guests visit Disneyland Paris after having visited Walt Disney World in Florida – both resorts allow you to immerse yourself in the Disney magic but it is important to understand that the two locations are very different.

This chapter aims to help you explore these differences between the resorts. You will discover what makes the different locations unique, as well as why some aspects of the Parisian parks are better, and others are better in Florida.

**1 - Local customs** – According to the last available figures from Disneyland Paris, 51% of all visitors to the resort are French, about 14% are from the UK. Other countries that have a high number of guests include Spain and Italy. The resort therefore has an extremely high proportion of local European visitors, unlike Walt Disney World which has visitors from all corners of the world.

There are, therefore, many American customs and traditions which simply do not apply to a European audience. One of these is waiting in a queue line - many Europeans simply do not understand or practice queuing systems; it is not in their culture. Instead people will crowd around in a small group instead of an orderly line. That means that when a bus arrives it is a free-for-all and people rush for the doors with no regard for who has been waiting the longest. For characters that make random appearances in the parks, you can expect a crowd of parents pushing their children to get their photo taken first.

Tipping for services is also very different. All meals in France have a tip automatically included in the price of the food, as such there is no need to tip extra unless you wish to. This compares to the US where tips of 15% to 20% of a meal's price are expected.

In general, the guests are much more disrespectful at the Parisian parks – they will climb into cordoned off areas, sit just about anywhere they can, and they smoke freely in the parks despite it being banned.

Guests in Europe expect to be able to have an alcoholic beverage with their meal – as such you will find beer on sale at all counter service locations. Wine is of course also offered at all table service locations. In general Europeans are more used to a culture of drinking alcohol with a meal than Americans, and the introduction of alcoholic drinks has not had a negative effect on the parks.

Last but not least, the European audience are a little bit more fashion conscious than the crowds that visit Florida. Ponchos are on sale at Disneyland Paris and are seen throughout the parks but they are more than often replaced by umbrellas and raincoats in Europe.

**2 - Languages** - All Cast Members (Disneyland Paris employees) must speak at least two major European languages, one of which must be French. Almost all of the Cast speaks English but it is not mandatory. You may very rarely encounter a Cast Member that does not speak English, so it pays to learn some basic French. If you go up arrogantly speaking English to a French person, they will not take it well. It is basic manners to learn some of the language when visiting another country and at least say "Bonjour", "Parlez-vous Anglais?" and "Merci" as a minimum.

**3 - The Cast Members** - The Cast Members in Florida and California, for the most part, will go above and beyond your requests, are extremely polite, will never be rude to a guest, have a passion for Disney and will do everything to make your stay as magical as possible. However, the Cast Members in the US are very restricted by the Disney rulebook, which even affects their personal lives such as how they can cut their hair.

When visiting Disneyland Paris, you will find a Disney Park for the 21st century where the 'Disney Look' that states how employees must look is deemed illegal by the state. The French employment laws are much more strict for employers meaning Cast Members cannot be reprimanded for not smiling or for leaning whilst at work.

In addition, French customer service is almost non-existent when compared to American, or even British, standards. Having said this, 99% of the cast are extremely pleasant, inviting and helpful and will help you as much as possible – just do not expect American customer service standards in France.

The Cast Members are generally very international and speak several languages, and if you want to meet people from all across Europe and the world, talk to the Cast Members and find out about their exciting journeys. Having a chat with one of the Cast from the resort for example could lead to you booking your next vacation to somewhere you would never thought of visiting in Europe.

**4 - The Size of the Resort** - This is the main difference between Walt Disney World and Disneyland Paris. Walt Disney World is 47 square miles or 121 square kilometres. In comparison, Disneyland Paris is 22.3 square kilometres. Walt Disney World is more than five times the size of Disneyland Paris. The difference is staggering: in fact all of Disneyland Paris could comfortably fit inside the parking lot for Magic Kingdom Park in Florida.

From the furthest resort hotels to the parks is no more than a 20-minute walk at Disneyland Paris or a five-minute bus journey, whereas at Walt Disney World it can be a 25-minute bus journey to a park and most distances you simply cannot walk. At Disneyland Paris, it is a five-minute walk between the two theme parks, and a five-minute walk to the Disney Village (a miniature version of Downtown Disney in Florida) from the parks.

The advantage of Disneyland Paris' small size is that you can walk throughout the whole resort, you can visit any of the other hotels easily and you will spend less time on traveling around and spend more time enjoying yourself instead. The disadvantage is that there are no water parks, there are less hotels to choose from and crucially there are fewer theme parks (there are only two in Paris, as opposed to four in Florida) – overall, there are much fewer things to do at Disneyland Paris.

Looking at the parks, Disneyland Park is slightly bigger than Magic Kingdom Park, but with more emptier, quieter areas and less rides – the walkways in the park feel significantly less crowded in Paris. Walt Disney Studios Park in Paris is much smaller that Disney's Hollywood Studios in Orlando. The resort hotels are also generally significantly smaller than their Floridian counterparts.

**5 - The Detail of the Parks** - Disneyland Park is absolutely beautiful and arguably the most beautiful theme park anywhere in the world - everything is just perfect from the castle to Frontierland, to Discoveryland, to Adventureland - it is all incredibly elaborately themed, sharing inspiration from the US parks whilst introducing exotic elements that cannot be found elsewhere. The hotels at Disneyland Paris are all American-themed but in our opinion still do not live up to the resort hotels found at Walt Disney World – the hotels in Paris are really just hotels whereas you could spend a whole day at several of the hotel resorts in the US and just enjoy the surroundings and experiences on offer.

In comparison, Walt Disney Studios Park is a shame of a park – it is filled with concrete and metallic structures everywhere, with very few thematic details. Although, over the past five years there has been an effort to improve the parks with new attractions and more heavily themed areas, it is clear that Walt Disney Studios Park lacks the detail that makes Disney theme parks unique. Even Hollywood Studios, which in our opinion is the worst themed park at Walt Disney World, has vastly superior theming to the Walt Disney Studios Park in Paris and more attractions.

**6 - Amazing unique shows and rides** - Disneyland Paris has some great unique rides and shows that just cannot be found at Walt Disney World. In Disneyland Park *Phantom Manor*, is a beautiful rendition of the classic Haunted Mansion ride with a new storyline and an entirely different interior but with some familiar elements; *Pirates of the Caribbean* is much longer, has a better queue line, new scenes and bigger drops at Disneyland Paris; *Space Mountain: Mission 2* is beautiful in Paris from the outside and it is an incredibly intense rollercoaster inside. It blows its Floridian counterpart out of the water; *Big Thunder Mountain* is great fun in Paris and is set in the middle of an island. Furthermore, there are lots of unique walkthroughs such as *Nautilus* too. *Casey Junior* and *Storybook Canal Boats* also do not exist in Florida. If you fancy the original *Star Tours* attraction, Disneyland Paris has that too. *Indiana Jones et le Temple du Peril* is also a unique rollercoaster at the resort. There is however no 'New Fantasyland expansion' in Paris. The *Disney Dreams* nighttime spectacular is like a mix of all of Walt Disney World's three nighttime shows rolled into one.

In Walt Disney Studios, *Crush's Coaster* is a unique spinning rollercoaster in the dark; *Cars Quatre Roues Rallye* is a unique spinning attraction; *The Art of Disney Animation* is different in Paris, if admittedly more basic; *Toy Story Playland* has three unique rides, and *Animagique* and *Cinemagique* are incredible stage shows not featured elsewhere. *Stitch Live* is a cool interactive show too. *Ratatouille: The Adventure* is a world-class never-before-seen ride unlike anything in the American parks.

**6 – You are not so locked in** - Right there on Disneyland Paris property, just two minutes from the park entrance, you can hop on a public transport high speed TGV train to other parts of France. Alternatively, in just 40 minutes you can use the regional RER trains and travel into central Paris and experience one of the most beautiful cities in the world.

You can also drive from your hotel and be at a non-Disney location in just a couple of minutes too. Disneyland Paris is all very self-contained so if you do fancy escaping the magic, it is easy to do so there unlike in Florida! For some people this freedom is a benefit, for others they prefer the Floridian immersion of the Disney magic.

**7 - Pricing** - Stays at Disneyland Paris can be very, very pricy as far as accommodation is concerned. Generally room prices will include tickets to the theme parks for the length of your stay. You will not find a room at a Disney hotel for under £200 or $300 per night – and these are the absolute cheapest rooms during off-peak seasons. In contrast, the cheapest hotels in Walt Disney World are one third of this price or less, though park tickets are not included. At Disneyland Paris, there are almost always special offers available so make sure to not book at full rack rate.

A one day entry ticket to Disneyland Paris for one park is €73 (£58 or $95) for adults and €63 for children. A park hopper is €88 (£70 or $114) and €66 respectively. The daily rate drastically reduces the longer you visit the resort.

For comparison, at Walt Disney World a one day, 1 park adult ticket is $108 dollars with tax, or a park hopper is $144 plus tax. In general, Walt Disney World is slightly more expensive for day tickets though it is true that there is more to do in the theme parks there. Long-term stays of 7 or 14-days in Florida become incredibly cheap per day.

Food prices at Disneyland Paris, however, are ridiculously expensive in comparison to the US and many people bring picnic food into the parks for this reason. A burger, fries and drink combo will set you back about €14 (£11/ $18) at Disneyland Paris per person. A burger and fries in the US will cost you about $11 without a drink or about $14 with one. This adds up to a big price difference when ordering for a family of four over several days.

**8 - Fastpasses** – Fastpass at Disneyland Paris works in the same way the paper Fastpass system worked in Walt Disney World. Florida's paper Fastpass system was replaced by the digital Fastpass+ system in 2014. At Disneyland Paris the return time windows are only 30 minutes long instead of the 1-hour in the US parks due to the smaller distances that you will need to cover between parks and rides.

**9 – Weather** – Florida is known for being the sunshine state and in general this is true, you can expect temperatures of about 30 degrees Celsius and 80 to 90 degrees Fahrenheit throughout most of the year. There are occasions where there are cold snaps and the temperatures drop drastically for a few days but nothing to the levels that are seen in Paris. Paris weather is much more variable; the average temperature in Paris in July and August is about 25 degrees Celsius (77 degrees Fahrenheit) whereas temperatures in January and February average at 3 degrees Celsius (37 in Fahrenheit).

Visitors to Walt Disney World throughout most of the year will have to deal with Hurricane season (June to November) when weather can get extreme, and tornados are also possible. These are extremely rare in Paris. Orlando visitors also deal with a tropical climate where thunderstorms are likely almost every day in the summer, closing all outdoor attractions and drenching anyone who is not prepared. Paris rain is much more unpredictable, though it is present year-round.

That concludes our look at the differences between the two resorts. This analysis may make the Parisian resort sound negative but do not be dissuaded from visiting Disneyland Paris because of some of the comparisons made here! Disneyland Paris is still the most beautiful Disney resort, it has dozens of unique rides, the atmosphere is magical and you will have a great time. Just be aware of the differences mentioned in this section and you will be prepared for a trip of a lifetime.

Chapter 20
# Seasonal Changes & The Future

In order to give its guests something different throughout the year, Disneyland Paris has seasonal and special events that celebrate traditions such as St. Patrick's Day, Halloween and Christmas. This section explores all of these special events that happen throughout the year.

Once you have discovered what lies ahead throughout 2015, take a look at what is in store for the future of the resort.

## St. David's Welsh Festival:

6$^{th}$ to 8$^{th}$ March 2015 and 4$^{th}$ to 6$^{th}$ March 2016

This three day long mini-season has been traditionally celebrated in Frontierland, at Disneyland Park. During the Festival guests can take photos with some of their favourite Disney characters clad in traditional Welsh robes.

In addition, Disneyland Paris usually has traditional Welsh singers such as a choir perform at the festival several times throughout the day.

Traditional music, a crafts market, traditional food and drink, complimentary face painting, and a special St. David's fireworks display also make up part of the festival.

## St. Patrick's Day:

**17th March 2015 and 17th March 2016**
Much like the St. David's day celebrations featured above, this one-day celebration of all things Celtic takes place in Frontierland, at Disneyland Park. Guests can enjoy live traditional music, photo opportunities, character appearances, a pre-parade, and a special St. Patrick's Day fireworks display.

## Swing into Spring:

**1st March to 31st May 2015**

179

In 2014, Disneyland Paris launched a new mini season called "Swing into Spring" where the park was overrun with almost 100,000 extra flowers, extra entertainment and more fun than ever. The new seasonal event was one of the most impressive new additions to the park we have seen in years with an incredible amount of new sights, smells and sounds for guests. This season returned in 2015 and was further enhanced from its 2014 debut. The information below relates to the 2015 edition of this event.

Inside Disneyland Park, Main Street USA station is adorned with the Swing into Spring logo inviting you into the park. In Town Square there are topiaries of Disney characters.

On Main Street USA the balconies are decorated with flowers all the way along the street. You will also be able to meet Rapunzel who will be back in the park for photo meet and greet opportunities. In Central Plaza, in front of the castle, you will find stunning topiaries of Disney characters.

The big show for the season, "Goofy's Garden Party", takes place several times per day. It is reasonably similar to 2014's "Disney's Spring Promenade" show which includes dancers and many Disney characters getting ready to celebrate spring.

"Minnie's Springtime Character Train" will also rock up with character favourites on board, and three cars decorated especially for the occasion are present too. Guests can see the White Rabbit (from Alice in Wonderland), as well as Thumper and Miss Bunny (from Bambi). Guests will be pleased to hear that Thumper and Miss Bunny will be available for meet-and-greet and photo opportunities too.

In the Disney Village there topiaries, as well as advice and workshops relating to plants.

The 2015 edition of the Swing into Spring season runs from 1$^{st}$ March to 31$^{st}$ May 2015.

# Frozen Summer:
1st June to 13th September 2015
In 2015, Disneyland Paris will launch its first themed summer season and what better way to do it than with movie-hit *Frozen*! The main event of the Frozen Summer celebration will be a Sing-a-Long spectacular featuring Anna and Elsa, in a new set in Frontierland's Chaparral Theatre. Shows will be presented 6 times a day in June and September, and 12 times per day in July and August. We expect this show to be *very* popular.

Right next-door to the theatre, is the Cottonwood Creek Ranch which hosts Arendelle's market filled with Frozen-themed delights.

Three times a day Anna and Elsa will come out in their royal coach and parade through the park, and in the evenings, the nighttime spectacular Disney Dreams will include a Frozen section. Magical!

# Halloween:

1st October to 1st November 2015.
Disneyland Paris' Halloween season is one of the most developed celebrations at the resort, with unique shows, parades, decors and more sure to delight guests. Although elements do change yearly, the season usually lasts for the whole of October as well as a few days of November.

The information provided below pertains to the 2014 Halloween season and will give you a general understanding of what you can expect, though some of these events may not be present in the 2015 Halloween season, and new events will undoubtedly be added. It is clear that the 2014 edition of Halloween had a heavy emphasis on the character of Maleficent due to the film of the same name being released in 2014 – we expect the villains to return in 2015 but with less of a focus on maleficent herself.

**New for 2014: The Maleficent Villains Happening** – This event takes place on Central Plaza in front of the castle and consists of the villains coming out from under the castle, parading around central plaza and then returning into their hiding places. It is a good way to get photos of all the villains in one place but is just a very small 5 minute happening with no meet and greet opportunities.

**New for 2014: Maleficent Courtyard** – The courtyard area at the back courtyard of Sleeping Beauty Castle is where Maleficent and other villains will gather throughout the day and night. Here there is a short show by maleficent, followed by several of the villains coming out. After 30 minutes, the characters go away and they are replaced by others.

**Mickey's Halloween Cavalcade Celebration** – This mini-parade themed around autumn and harvesting passes Sleeping Beauty Castle and Main Street USA several times per day. See Mickey, Minnie and many other characters and dancers in autumnal colours. New for 2014 is the addition of Daisy who will open the parade, as well as a new float featuring the three little pigs, Horace Horsecollar and Clarabelle Cow. Disney Magic on Parade continues to also be performed once per day.

**Decorations** – Main Street USA will be invaded by ghostly decorations making for some great photo opportunities. Frontierland will also be decorated with spooky delights. Disney characters will also sport Halloween-themed costumes throughout the parks.

**Minnie's Costume Couture** – Meet Minnie in her dedicated meet and greet location located by Casey's Corner on Main Street USA. Stitch will also be present at this photo location to meet guests.

**Goofy's Candy Factory** – Goofy is clad in his Halloween gear in Town Square, ready to take photos with you by his new Trick or Treat candy machine.

**Jack and Sally's Cemetery** (from The Nightmare Before Christmas) – Meet Jack and Sally at their Halloween themed meet and greet location in Frontierland.

**Disney's Halloween Party** – Taking place on the 31$^{st}$ October 2015 itself between 8:30pm and 1:00am, this separate ticketed event offers an evening of frightening entertainment and hellish surprises. Most park attractions will be open during the event and guests may wear Halloween costumes subject to certain restrictions. Entry is charged at £35/€42 for the evening for guests aged 3 and over. Guests aged under 3 years old get free admission. Guests may enter the park from 5:00pm with their Halloween Party ticket.

## Mickey's Magical Fireworks and Bonfire:
2nd, 4th and 6th November 2015

Expect the night sky to be transformed above Lake Disney (located by the Disney hotels - no park ticket is required for admission into this area) as Disney sets its fireworks off to music to celebrate Bonfire Night. The 2014 show lasts approximately 20 minutes in length.

# Christmas:

## 7th November 2015 to 7th January 2016

For the most magical time of the year, make Disneyland Paris your stop. Here you are guaranteed snow every day, magical characters and unforgettable experiences. The following details are for the 2014 Christmas season. Traditionally, the Christmas seasons do not change hugely from year to year so you can expect much of this information to be valid for the 2015 Christmas season too. Information on the 2015 season will not be unveiled before September 2015 at the very earliest.

**New for 2014**: Merida, the princess from Disney-Pizar's *Brave*, will finally arrive at Disneyland Paris. Guests will be able to meet and pose for photographs with Merida just next to Casey's Corner on Main Street, USA.

**New for 2014**: Another unforgettable Princess event will be the *Disney Princess Promenade* which we expect to be a short show in the style of the Spring and Summer shows which have taken place throughout 2014. Exact details were not available at the time of going to press.

**New for 2014**: Guests will be able meet the stars of *Frozen*, Anna and Elsa for the very first time at the Princess Pavilion in Fantasyland.

Christmas at Disneyland Paris will also include unique shows, a 24-metre tall Christmas tree, decorations everywhere, a meet and greet with Father Christmas in his Christmas village, and Disney characters in seasonal costumes.

A Christmas parade also made its debut in 2014 featuring floats from the Christmas cavalcade which ran in both 2012 and 2013, as well as new additions. This parade was performed three times per day, and replaced *Disney Magic on Parade* completely during the Christmas season.

Every evening as the night falls, the signature Christmas tree will come to life in "Magical Christmas Wishes" as it is illuminated with its almost one thousand decorations. We expect this show to be the same as what was offered last year - a light and sound show starring Jiminy Cricket and Pinocchio who will also make it snow on Main Street USA as well as illuminate the Christmas tree in all its glory.

To end the night, *Disney Dreams of Christmas* returns for the 2014 season. Here projections, water jets, special effects and pyrotechnics will bring Sleeping Beauty Castle to life with the help of Olaf the snowman from *Frozen*, as guests celebrate different Christmas traditions from around the world and see winter-themed scenes from Disney classics. The 2014 version of Disney Dreams of Christmas was a vastly improved version on the 2013 show, but we believe there will still be further changes as the spectacle is still far from perfect.

The Christmas spirit can even be extended into your accommodation in 2015. If you are staying at the Disneyland hotel, for a £136 per room supplement you can have a Christmas themed room with festive decorations, a Christmas tree and small gifts for you to keep. The same is available at the Hotel New York for £103.

In Europe Christmas Eve and New Year's Eve dinners are a big family affair which Disney aims to capitalise on. As such dinners on these days are available at a heavy supplement. Prices vary from £89 (€129) to £211 (€259) per adult on Christmas Eve. On Christmas day a special 4-course lunch is available for £139 per adult. Child prices are available on request from Disneyland Paris but in the past have been less than half the price of an adult. New Year's Eve meals range in price from £97 (€119) to £243 (€299) per adult.

Full details on these meals are available over the phone or in the latest Disneyland Paris brochure. Personally we think these prices are ludicrous with a family of 4 spending at least €400 minimum on a single meal. Our recommendation is to eat early (before 7:00pm) in one of the quick service restaurants to avoid these hefty price tags (or a table service location as a late lunch), choose from one of the table service restaurants not doing special dinners, or eat in the Disney Village at selected restaurants.

## New Year's Eve
### 31st December
Celebrate the start of the New Year at Disneyland Paris. This is traditionally the busiest day at the resort and you can expect the theme parks to reach maximum capacity and for there to be very long wait times. If you can put up with that, you can experience a fireworks display at Disneyland Park, at Walt Disney Studios Park and at Lake Disney (with no admission cost at this last location). The theme parks are open until 1:00am on New Year's Eve meaning you have one hour of post-fireworks attraction time if you wish to take advantage of this.

# The Future – Projects in progress and rumours:

**Walt Disney Studios Park Expansion** - Walt Disney studios Park is due to continue to expand with additional attractions, and area. It is even possible that the entire theme park get a re-theme though nothing has been confirmed in regards to this. Some of the projects that are rumoured to arrive include Toy Story Midway Mania, and a re-theme of the entire Backlot area to Marvel. A new attraction will not open in the park during 2015 as there is currently no construction taking place. It is possible that construction for a new attraction may begin in 2015, however, and open during 2016 or later.

**Disneyland Park Refurbishments** – Disneyland Park has not had a new attraction for many years and the park will therefore be going through a big refurbishment program to get all the attractions up to date and looking new for the resort's 25$^{th}$ anniversary in 2017. The closure of **Space Mountain: Mission 2** has been confirmed and runs from 12$^{th}$ January 2015 to 24$^{th}$ July 2015. **Videopolis Theatre** and **Café Hyperion** will also close until 11$^{th}$ July 2015.

Other attractions that are set to close sometime in 2015 or 2016 for a lengthy refurbishment as confirmed by Disneyland Paris include: Animagique, Star Tours and Peter Pan's Flight.

We had been provided with the following lengthy closure dates by a reliable insider but as these have not been confirmed, do take these with a pinch of salt. It's a small world will be closed from 27$^{th}$ July 2015 to 18$^{th}$ December 2015, Adventure Isle will close from 31$^{st}$ August 2015 to 29$^{th}$ April 2016, and Big Thunder Mountain will close from 2$^{nd}$ November 2015 to 16$^{th}$ December 2016.

**New Shows** - A Star Wars themed Jedi Training Academy will launch in Summer 2015 at Videopolis Theatre in Discoveryland. Summer 2015 will also see a Frozen-themed show come to the Chaparral theatre. The arrival of both of these shows has been confirmed by Disneyland Paris.

**Disney Village expansion** – Disney Village is to be expanded over the coming years with new shopping and dining experiences though no firm plans have been announced. A new hotel is equally being considered although it is unclear where this will be located.

**Technological updates throughout the resort** – Disneyland Paris is committed to keeping up with the times, and is working on an integrated system which will eventually culminate in an RFID card for guests – there are no specific details on this but if this is anything like the project at Walt Disney World this could mean that guests will be able to use only one card to enter the parks, pay for dinner and merchandise with, have electronic dining credits and open their hotel room door. No date for this RFID card system has currently been announced. In addition, free public Wi-Fi is due to be introduced at both parks at some point in 2015.

**Hotel refurbishments** – Disneyland Paris has been refurbishing all of its hotels over the past years. Disney's Newport Bay Club is currently undergoing this process and this is expected to be completed at some point in 2015. After the Newport Bay Club, Disney's Hotel New York will be closing in its entirety for a year for its refurbishment. We expect this closure to begin in Spring of 2016 and last until the Spring of 2017.

## You have reached the end!

If you have made it this far, thank you very much for reading everything – we hope this guide has made a big difference to your trip to Disneyland Paris and that you have found some tips that will save you time, money and hassle! Remember to take this guide with you whilst you are visiting the resort.

To contact us, email us at info@dlparisguide.com. If you have any corrections, feedback about any element of the guide, or a review of a ride or restaurant - send us an email and we will get back to you! You could even help contribute to the ride and show reviews we will be including in future editions of this guide.

Please use our special affiliate links mentioned throughout this guide when booking, as these help us keep going at no extra cost to you. Thanks!

We also encourage you to leave a review on Amazon or wherever you have purchased this guide from. Your reviews make a huge difference in helping other people find this guide. Thank you.

If you have enjoyed this guide you will want to check out **The Independent Guide to Universal Orlando 2015**, **The Independent Guide to Disneyland 2015** and **The Independent Guide to Walt Disney World 2015.** Also keep an eye out for **The Independent Guide to Orlando 2015**. All of these guidebooks are available right now! You will find detailed information on every ride, show and attraction and more insider tips that will save you hours in line!

Have a magical stay!

**Photo credits:**
The following photos have been used from Flickr (unless otherwise stated) in this guide under a Creative Commons license. Thank you to: 'Alias 0591' (Disney Dreams), Loren Javier (Crush's Coaster, Buffalo Bill's), David Jafra (Disneyland Hotel, Earl of Sandwich, Flying Carpets, Star Tours, Parachute Drop, Tower of Terror, Catastrophe Canyon, Lancelot's Carrousel), 'Sparkly Kate' (Sequoia Lodge), Sean MacEntee (Newport Bay Club, Rock n Rollercoaster), 'Doggettx (Main Street USA), 'flightlog' (Big Thunder Mountain, Cars), Wikimedia (Casey Jr.), Jeremy Thompson (Riverboat Landing, Temple du Peril, Peter Pan's Flight, Les Voyages de Pinocchio, Dumbo: The Flying Elephant), Victor R. Ruiz (Phantom Manor), and 'Hamilton of Forbes' (Wild West Show).

Printed in Great Britain
by Amazon.co.uk, Ltd.,
Marston Gate.